THE CONSOLATION
OF THE WILD

Other books by Walt McLaughlin:

Seven Thousand Miles to Nowhere
Hitchhiking across North America in the Seventies

Campfire Philosophy
Fragments from a Field Journal

The Great Wild Silence
Ruminations and Excursions in the Adirondacks

A Reluctant Pantheism
Discovering the Divine in Nature

Cultivating the Wildness Within

The Impossible Cosmos
A Year of Amateur Astronomy and Big Questions

The Unexpected Trail
Taking on the 100 Mile Wilderness

Forest under my Fingernails
Reflections and Encounters on the Long Trail

The Allure of Deep Woods
Backpacking the Northville-Placid Trail

Arguing with the Wind
A Journey into the Alaskan Wilderness

Backcountry Excursions
Venturing into the Wild Regions of the Northeast

Loon Wisdom
Sounding the Depths of Wildness

THE CONSOLATION
OF THE WILD

Grief, Hardship and Happiness
on the Cohos Trail

by

Walt McLaughlin

Wood Thrush Books

Published by Wood Thrush Books
            27 Maple Grove Estates
            Swanton, Vermont 05488

ISBN 978-1-7345175-4-5

*In memory of my parents
Margaret and G. James McLaughlin,
and Matika, wilderness dog.*

Preface

For decades I have ventured into the backcountry of the northeast and have written at length about my wild encounters and even wilder musings there. This comes easy to me. In fact, it's hard for me go backpacking, take a short hike, or even fish a stream these days without feeling an urge to recount it. But this narrative is the first time that I have included the emotional turmoil that comes with losing a loved one. To say that I am out of my comfort zone while writing about grief would be a gross understatement.

A few days ago my wife Judy read this narrative and approved of it. As a certified end-of-life doula who is no stranger to death and dying, her opinion means a lot to me. She had her reservations about my story, though. While she applauded me for writing about grief, she felt that I had held back, that I should have delved deeper into the nitty-gritty of it. I am somewhat relieved by her assessment. I was afraid that I had ruined this story by talking about grief at all. What place does such a thing have in an outdoor/nature narrative? Judy reminded me that few things are more natural than death. Nature is rife with it.

Along with facing the death of loved ones, I also faced my own mortality during this trip. That is, I was a sixty-something fellow trying to hike like someone half my age. That didn't work out so well for me. My body let me know that I had screwed up. More to the point, I became acutely aware of my body's physical limitations. That was eye opening to say the least.

All this said, I enjoyed being on the move, hiking a relatively new trail system that I imagine will be quite popular someday. Northern New Hampshire is remote, wild country, and that's what I like most. Deep woods solitude is what I hope to experience whenever I go alone into the forest, and the Cohos Trail provided plenty of that along with magnificent mountain views, beautiful ponds and dreamy meadows. In that regard, I couldn't have asked for a better trip.

Mother Nature sent me mixed messages during this outing to be sure. At times I was so miserable that I seriously questioned why I was putting myself through all this. Other times I experienced those ecstatic moments that keep me going back to the wild for more. This hike was an emotional roller coaster ride, chock full of grief, hardship and happiness. I could have written a simpler, more upbeat narrative but didn't want to whitewash what actually happened. As Gary Snyder once said, "Life in the wild is not just eating berries in the sunlight." Granted, my grief made a tough hike even more difficult, but I found the Cohos Trail well worth doing even under less-than-ideal circumstances. Seasoned backpackers who love the wild, and want to get off the beaten path for a change, should definitely give it a try.

– Walt McLaughlin
December 2020

THE CONSOLATION
OF THE WILD

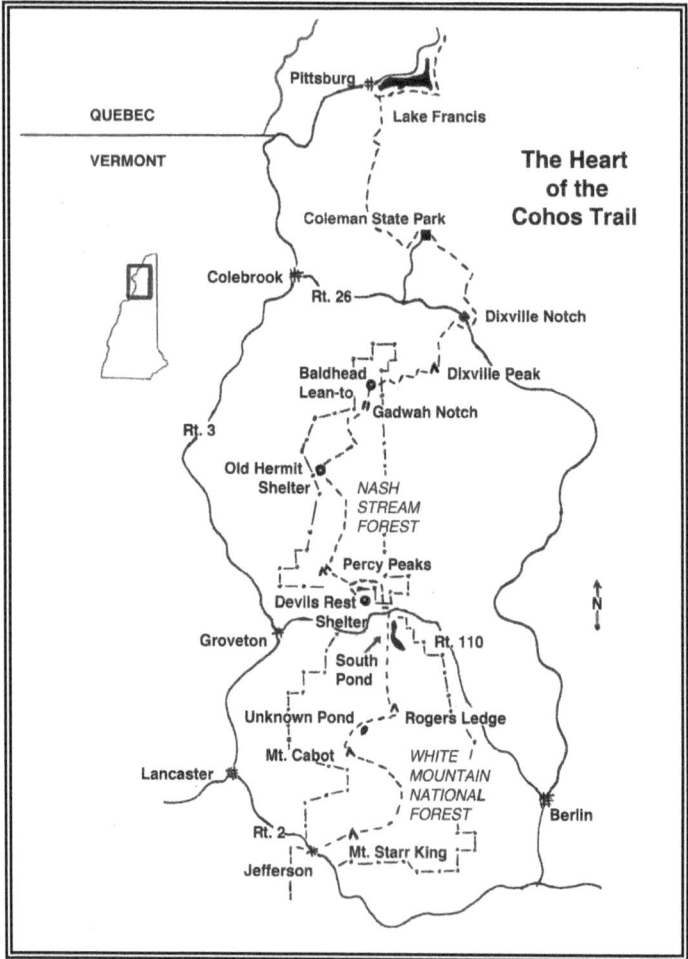

The Heart
of the
Cohos Trail

QUEBEC

VERMONT

Pittsburg

Lake Francis

Coleman State Park

Colebrook

Rt. 26

Dixville Notch

Baldhead
Lean-to

Dixville Peak

Gadwah Notch

Rt. 3

Old Hermit
Shelter

NASH
STREAM
FOREST

Percy Peaks

Devils Rest
Shelter

Rt. 110

Groveton

South
Pond

Unknown Pond

Rogers Ledge

Mt. Cabot

WHITE
MOUNTAIN
NATIONAL
FOREST

Lancaster

Berlin

Rt. 2

Mt. Starr King

Jefferson

N

1.

The long wait is over. A hike stuck for years in the planning stage is beginning right now. Trekking poles dig into the gravel road as I press forward with a fully loaded pack tugging at my shoulders. A couple minutes ago, after hugs and kisses, my wife Judy hopped back into her car and sped away. Now I'm on my own, ready to do an 80-mile section of the Cohos Trail from Jefferson to Pittsburg, New Hampshire. It'll be no small feat for this 63-year-old hiker. I'm both excited and apprehensive about the prospect. The mountain range directly ahead is formidable and my body is not in the best shape. But a window of opportunity has opened up and I am seizing it. I have managed to set aside, at least temporarily, all my concerns and responsibilities back in the lowlands. For the next eleven days, I will be a woods walker, a denizen of the mountains, a wild man and nothing more.

      The trailhead parking lot at the end of the short access road is full of cars. It's a cool, partly cloudy

Saturday in the middle of June and there's a summit with great views directly ahead, so I shouldn't be surprised. All the same, there was no one here when I scouted this trailhead five days ago. Hmm.... This outing may not be the immersion into deep forest solitude that I had hoped it would be. Then again, the crowd will probably thin out considerably once I get beyond day-hiker range. That's usually the case.

A little after noon I charge up the trail, setting my sights on the top of Mt. Starr King less than three miles away. Then I remind myself that it's a 2,400-foot climb to that summit. Better cut my pace and conserve energy. I stop once to slather on bug dope, when the black flies become menacing. I stop a second time to tie a bandana around my forehead, when beads of sweat start dripping from it. A short while later, I stop a third time to catch my breath and take in my surroundings. The humidity is high in these wet woods, and the trail underfoot is muddy. The leaves of birches, maples and other hardwood trees are a bright vernal green thanks to persistent rainfall the past few months. Foamflower, blue violets, false Solomon's seal and other late spring wildflowers are still in bloom, scattered amid ferns and hobblebush. Sunbeams break through the canopy, illuminating the shaded understory here and there. It's an enchanting interplay of shadow and light. A stream roars through the deep ravine off to the left, washing away all thought of life beyond the forest. An earthy yet refreshing smell of growth and decay fills the air, along with the sweet perfume of fresh pollen. God it feels good to be here! I raise a water bottle to my lips and gulp down as much water as I can before moving on.

A pair of hikers passes me on their way downhill. Then another couple comes along, then a few more people. I count eight groups descending before losing track. Looks like most of the day hikers got an early start, have reached the summit already, and are on their way down. A twenty-something man and his mother pass me on their way up the mountain. They're moving fast. She's complaining about the bugs. An older couple, also going uphill, passes me while I'm negotiating a particularly steep, rocky section of trail. They're from Florida, they say, and were falsely told that this would be an easy hike. I can't help but laugh at that. Then I wish them good luck.

My trekking poles click against rocks as I slowly make my way up the mountain, putting one foot in front of another, breathing heavily. No reason to rush, I keep telling myself. I have all afternoon to reach the summit. Once again I stop to catch my breath and drink water. A chipmunk scurries across the trail right in front of me. A hummingbird appears out of nowhere, darting back and forth then disappearing just as quickly. A veery calls out, then a nuthatch *meep-meeps*. A tufted titmouse sings. The forest is alive yet peaceful, quiet compared to the developed lowlands. My nerves uncoil with each step I take.

The Cohos Trail is a 170-mile, relatively new footpath stretching north from the trailhead of the Davis Path in the heart of the White Mountains all the way to the Canadian border. Unlike the many trails in the magnificent yet very busy Presidential Range, few people travel the CT or even know about it. Beyond the Whites, the Cohos Trail enters the Great North Woods – the largely ignored northern tip of New Hampshire where moose and bear thrive, and towns are few and far between. The CT passes through some of the most remote country in the Northeast. That's how it caught my attention, and why I have wanted to hike it for quite some time.

Originally I had planned on hiking 62 miles from Jefferson to Dixville Notch in nine or ten days, doing what I believe to be the wildest part of the Cohos Trail. But the length and duration of this hike grew a couple months ago, when it became apparent that it was really going to happen. What the hell, I figured, might as well make it count since there's no telling when I'll be able to do something like this again. After all, ten years have slipped away since my last big solo hike. Life, with all its demands, distractions and detours, seems to get in the way of the best laid plans.

An easy-to-miss sign points to the left, to a spring just off the trail. I follow a short path down to a small, shallow pool at the base of a boulder. Then I pull out a water filter and start pumping. The sun breaks through the clouds as I fill all three of my bottles. I raise closed eyes to the sunlight while drinking half a liter of the cool, clear, life-sustaining liquid. Springs are one of the many delights of the trail. Water, so essential to survival, seems to be sweetest where it first emerges from the ground. And the warm light caressing my face feels heavenly.

Back on the trail, the discouraged older couple from Florida is on their way down. They haven't gone much farther uphill than the spring. The woman who had been complaining about the bugs is soon on their heels, shortly after tagging the summit. Her twenty-something son has kept going to Mt. Waumbek, another mile away. I keep chugging along, pushing myself upward and taking short breaks as needed.

Now well above 3,000 feet, the forest has changed dramatically, with spruce and fir replacing the hardwoods. There's more moss than anything else on the forest floor. It's a different kind of wild beauty to be sure. I look around, grooving on the boreal forest as I walk. Suddenly my left boot slips off a wet rock and down I go to one knee. The weight of my backpack forces me farther downward in a slow motion fall until I plant my face in the ground. I get back up, muddy and chagrined, with a bleeding cut on my forearm. But I'm not seriously injured. I brush off the mud then keep going. "Be careful," I scold myself out loud, "Pay attention." Can't afford to lose my mobility out here. And with that thought, I finish the ascent at a deliberately slower pace.

I reach the summit of Starr King four hours after starting my ascent – a surprisingly slow rate of travel. But here I am. After leaning my pack against a rock, I walk over to an opening in the trees to enjoy the view. The Presidential Range looms in the distance, dominating the southern horizon beneath a mostly blue sky. I snap a photo of it with my camera then sit on a rocky outcropping to rest. I pull out my map to see what the trail looks like between here and Mt. Waumbek. The twenty-something fellow, just now returning from that summit, assures me that it isn't difficult. He chats with me a short while before catching up to his mother, who is already well on her way down the mountain. Then I'm alone in the clearing. Just a few gray jays and me, I should say. They swoop to the ground right in front of me, making all kinds of noise as they prance about. They are entertaining, certainly, but their begging is a little over the top so I try to ignore them. That's easier said than done. When I look away, they make even more noise.

Two physically fit, middle-aged fellows in athletic gear suddenly appear. No doubt they just did the climb in a couple of hours. They are breathing heavily but not winded. They pull out cell phones and snap pictures of the Presidential Range, admiring its rugged beauty. Then they strike up a conversation with me. But I have to go. It's getting late. I need to get on the other side of Waumbek and make camp before the sun goes down. So I excuse myself after a brief exchange of pleasantries and slip away, venturing farther north.

2.

The trail beyond Mt. Starr King turns east while dropping sharply to a narrow path full of roots, rocks and mud holes. Then it climbs up Mt. Waumbek. I don't lose much elevation in the process but the final ascent is tiring all the same. It has been a long afternoon. After doing the mile of ridgeline between the summits, I cross over the wooded 4,000-foot Mt. Waumbek. A short break at a lookout on the other side, then I am searching for a place to make camp.

Waumbek's eastern shoulder is flat enough, but it is thick with spruce and fir both standing and fallen. Eventually I find a spot to make camp about twenty yards off the trail. It's a mound barely big enough to sleep on, surrounded by saplings. It'll have to do. I clear away some downed, half-rotten branches then set up my tarp, tying its guy lines to nearby trees and planted trekking poles. My mosquito bar, a rectangular piece of netting designed to cover a camper's cot, goes underneath. I tie its guy lines to the corners of the tarp.

When I'm done I have a cozy little haven from bugs with a steep enough pitch to shed rain. And shedding rain is important. The sky is beginning to cloud over.

Dinner is an expedient affair because the bugs have become annoying in the suddenly still air. No breaking out my stove and boiling up water. Besides, this is a dry camp. Have to conserve water. I eat handfuls of trail mix and sesame sticks, along with an energy bar washed down with a cup of water flavored with lemonade powder. With my belly full enough, I tie my food bag to a line stretched between two trees. Then I raise it out of bear's reach. One last cup of water to brush my teeth and clean up a bit then I crawl under the tarp. That leaves two liters of water for tomorrow morning. The next dependable water source is three miles away.

Low clouds pelt the tarp with raindrops as I snuggle into my sleeping bag and write in a field journal by headlamp. It's only drizzle. With any luck it won't become a downpour. The wind suddenly picks up, rocking the trees overhead. The air temperature, comfortably in the 60s most of the day, is falling fast now. I pull a heavy thermal shirt out of my clothes bag. Might need it later tonight. Camped at nearly 4,000 feet on a mountain ridge, I'm feeling a little exposed.

What a day this has been! A good start to the trek. Up on the Kilkenny Ridge Trail and looking at four summits and ten miles tomorrow. I'm tired and sore but no worse for wear. Hope to get a good night's sleep.

In 2009, I hiked the 100-Mile Wilderness in northern Maine – a challenging section of the Appalachian Trail just south of Mount Katahdin. I hiked it southbound with my long-haired German shepherd, Matika, limping out at Monson after twelve days on the trail. When my wife picked me up, I told her that this was my last big trek, that I'd had enough of it. But she didn't believe me, and for good reason. The next day, before we even got back to our home state of Vermont, I felt the urge again. As Judy drove Route 2, cutting through the northern part of New Hampshire's White Mountains, I gazed out the passenger's window at the forested mountains rising sharply away from the road. Suddenly I wanted to roam through that wild, remote country because, well, because it's there.

The writer Diane Ackerman calls it "deep play." She borrowed the phrase from the Utilitarian philosopher Jeremy Bentham who dismissed any activity as deep play when "the stakes are so high that… it is irrational for anyone to engage in it at all." Ackerman turned the phrase around, giving it a somewhat different meaning. To her an activity becomes deep play "when it starts focusing one's life and offering ecstatic moments." Deep play usually involves the sacred. That is, it engages one's entire being, and has the potential to alter one's worldview. Yes, the stakes are high but it's worth it in ways that can't be rationally understood. And that best explains the urge I so often feel to venture alone for a week or so into wild country. I don't recommend it, but I don't want to give it up either.

A few years after the 100-Mile Wilderness hike, I heard about a brand new trail system cutting through the very landscape I had gazed upon during that ride home from Maine. Soon thereafter, I acquired a book written by Kim Robert Nilsen simply called *The Cohos Trail*. Scrawled across the front of it: "162 miles of remote, wild and rugged hiking trail from the White Mountains to the Canadian border." Talk dirty to me! By the summer of 2014, I had cobbled together a plan to hike what seemed like the wildest, most interesting part of it, from the town of Jefferson on Route 2 to Dixville Notch – north of the busy Presidential Range yet south of the somewhat developed Connecticut Lakes region. I estimated that I could do that 62-mile section in eight or nine days, comfortably in ten. I would hike it the following summer.

With that rough plan in mind, I drove over to northern New Hampshire in late October to scout the Jefferson trailhead, the Dixville Notch exit, and the only road crossing: Route 110. My dog Matika went with me, of course. We ended up hiking a one-mile stretch of the Cohos Trail south out of South Ponds

Recreation Area just off Route 110. The parking lot was empty. A chilling wind knocked leaves to the ground as we hiked. Matika approved of the trail. So did I.

But life is what happens while we're busy making plans. In June 2015, with preparations underway to hike the CT the following August, I lost my job. It wasn't much of a job really – just a part-time clerk position in a UPS Store. But I wasn't quite ready to take the leap, turning a recently started online bookselling business into a fulltime venture. No matter. Business was off at the store and someone had to go. Since I was the old guy with a side business, my boss probably figured that I wouldn't be sticking around anyway. Suddenly I was scrambling to make my fledgling book biz a dependable source of income. Consequently, the CT hike was postponed indefinitely.

That same summer, my stepson Matthew sold his highly successful cyber security business in Virginia. A few months later, at his wife Joy's urging, he decided to "invest" in a house in Vermont so that Judy and I could live rent/mortgage free in our old age. A good son, taking care of his mother. A *very* generous offer. Judy was all for it. How could I say no? The house was built the following winter and spring, and we moved into it in June of 2016. Then came the rather challenging task of fixing up and selling off the 120-

year-old house that Judy and I owned. And that's what I did instead of hiking that summer.

The following year took me by surprise, even though I really should have seen it coming. In the spring of 2017, my 87-year-old mother ended up in rehab after falling down. She had all the symptoms of Parkinson's disease and was having trouble getting around. My 88-year-old father couldn't take care of her. He was frail and having his own trouble with dementia. I made a quick trip back to Ohio to help my sister and brothers sort things out. Mom went into a nursing home in July. A month later she was confused, combative and having psychotic episodes. I went back to Ohio again, when she was transferred to a psychiatric hospital. Eventually the doctors got her meds straightened out so Mom was able to think clearly again and return to the nursing home. I made a third trip back at Christmas just to make sure she was okay.

Meanwhile my canine hiking companion, Matika, started having trouble getting around. Judy and I suspected it was due to some kind of degenerative disease, but the vet said there's no test for that kind of thing. So I changed my plans that summer. My dog and I went for a short hike to a wilderness pond in the Adirondacks and hung out there instead of hiking the CT. Only a few days out of contact with the family. Considering the circumstances, it seemed like the right thing to do.

In 2018 I did a lot of *very* short hikes with Matika. She wasn't up for much else. I also made another trip back to Ohio see Mom. She had adjusted to life in the nursing home but her health was steadily declining. During the course of the year, we talked every Sunday over the phone, and sometimes again during the week. I didn't want to do anything that would put me out of touch with her for ten days. With that in mind, I hiked a section of the Appalachian Trail in northwestern New Hampshire with my old hiking buddy John Woodyard, keeping a cell phone handy. We had planned on doing 46 miles and six mountains in four days. It took us five. John was disappointed by our performance but I found it encouraging. Even now in my 60s, I could probably still do a 62-mile section of the Cohos Trail. Maybe more.

I needed to just do it, to go for a long solo hike again. Judy agreed. I was becoming difficult to live with. In December I resolved to hike the CT the following year, leaving Matika behind. My Mom's health was still a wild card, though. So I planned on trekking the CT in June and, if things took a turn for the worse back in Ohio, I would postpone the trip until late summer or fall. I'd carry a cell phone with me and leave the trail in the middle of the hike if necessary. Not the way I like to go into the woods, but it would have to do.

Now here it is, 2019. Five months ago, I started losing weight and training for the trip. I started hiking without my dog in order to get in shape, even though it felt like I was cheating on her. My primary care physician gave me a clean bill of health during an annual checkup. When I told her about my plan to hike the CT, she suggested that I take two zero days – days on the trail but *not* hiking – instead of one. I smiled at that, thinking it impractical, but told her that I would consider it.

I lost ten pounds right away but gained half of it back when I started eating nervously. A cold snap froze a pipe in the new house. Water flooded into the basement. It was a big mess. By the time I got all that cleaned up, Matika had become incontinent – a different kind of mess – and she was having a hard time walking at all. Then she stayed in her bed, obviously in pain. When it became clear to us that she was dying, Judy and I made what the vet called "the compassionate decision." In the middle of March, we held Matika in our arms as she was euthanized. Then suddenly I was alone every time I took a hike.

My book biz, which had been doing quite well for several years, went into a slump in February while I was dealing with the flood and my dying dog. That downturn continued into the spring. I tried not to worry, well aware that businesses large and small have their ups and downs. It became a concern only when my operating cash dried up. What I needed was a big infusion of new inventory, but I kept missing the best library book sales. Several big ones were happening in the end of April and early May. I had every intention of working them. That's when I got the news: Mom wasn't doing well.

Mom became less ambulatory, thinner and weaker through the winter. Curiously enough, she seemed to rally at Easter. Then all of a sudden she couldn't get out of bed. A few days later my sister Connie told me that Mom was nearing the end. I found that hard to believe. After all, Mom's health had taken a turn for the worse several times before and she had always bounced back. In fact, the health care workers at the nursing home called her The Comeback Kid. Then again, Mom had said a few things during our phone conversation at Easter that haunted me. No, it wasn't so much *what* she said but *how* she said those things, as if she was saying goodbye. Judy and I started packing our bags and clearing away work matters the day after I got word from my sister. That was a Friday in the end of April. Saturday morning early we were on the road, headed back to Ohio. We didn't get fifty miles down the road before Connie called again. She said that Mom had died during the night.

So this time, instead of going back to see Mom, Judy and I went back for a memorial service. We didn't stay long afterwards. On the way back home, we spent a night at Letchworth State Park. There I went for a short hike at daybreak and cried, finding some solace in roaring waterfalls. By the time we got home, I was down with a particularly nasty flu bug. That laid me low for two weeks. All the same, I was still determined to hike the CT. After recovering from the flu, I got serious about training and preparations. By then it was the middle of May.

For a month I walked and hiked as much I could, breaking in a brand new pair of boots with good ankle support and excellent tread. I acquired an updated map of the Cohos Trail and was surprised by all the changes on it. I bought a new rain cover for my backpack, as well. After all, a lot of rain had fallen recently. I carefully checked my gear, patching an old pair of hiking pants, reinforcing a frayed seam on my pack, and putting guy lines on a new tarp. Then I started provisioning, when I wasn't working on my book biz, puttering in the yard, slipping away to vacation with Judy for a few days, or attending a grandkid's graduation in Massachusetts. It was a juggling act to be sure.

Five days before starting the hike, I drove over to New Hampshire to recon the Jefferson trailhead, road crossings, and new finishing point, the town of Pittsburg on Lake Francis. Despite the fact that training had not gone well, I had added another day and 18 more miles to my hiking plan. In a fit of optimism, I drove to

Coleman State Park and paid $32 to reserve a campsite. There I would spend my last night on the trail. Last but not least, I drove deep into the Nash Stream Forest on a dusty, gravel road to cache some provisions. That way I wouldn't have to start the hike with all eleven days of food in my pack. A quarter mile up the trail from the dirt road, I shot a compass bearing due west then bushwhacked twenty-five yards into the forest. There I slung a waterproofed, 5-pound bag of food in the trees. I would pick it up on my way through.

While hanging that bag, I acquired a dozen black fly bites and a tick. That motivated me the next day to secure another bottle of 100% Deet insect repellent. Then I contacted my physician. She gave me a prescription for a few doses of a powerful antibiotic called Doxycycline, just in case I found a tick dug into my flesh during the hike. I immediately filled the prescription then squirreled away that medicine in my first aid kit, hoping it wouldn't be necessary. By Friday evening, yesterday that is, I was all stressed out by these last minute preparations but as ready as I could be for this trip. My food and gear was laid out neatly on the floor of my study, checked and double-checked. Early this morning, while Judy was still sleeping, I stuffed it all into a large, expedition backpack. It weighed 45 pounds, water included. Not too bad. I loaded the pack into the trunk of my wife's car, along with a pair of sturdy trekking poles. Then it was just a matter of getting to the trailhead.

3.

Daybreak. Dueling veerys and a chickadee awaken me. I open my eyes to see a thick mist hanging in the trees. I'm in the clouds. Slept well last night despite gusting wind and a light, steady rain. Now there's only the faint patter of a few droplets landing on the tarp. I'm achy all over despite the comfy pad beneath me. I raise the net and crawl away from the tarp, into a silent, still and dripping forest.

My legs cramp as I stand up. I shake it out then check myself for ticks. Nothing. That's good. The air is cool and damp so I waste no time getting dressed. After stepping away to pee, I stumble over to the food bag slung in the trees and retrieve it before returning to camp. I wash my face with water pooled in the lower corner of my tarp, conserving the two liters of water that I have on hand. No hot tea this morning. I'll just have an energy bar, break camp and go. Then I quickly change my mind. There are no bugs right now so why not fire up the stove and boil water for tea? The trail can wait.

While sipping tea and looking around, I marvel at how many dead spruce trees there are, those still standing as well as those on the ground. I recall reading a book a couple decades ago that addressed this issue. It was called *North Woods.* Peter Marchand, the author of that book, attributed the die-off to several variables, including "short- and long-term climactic fluctuations." I don't want to jump to any conclusions but I've noticed a lot of changes to wild country during the past forty years. Nowadays there are more mudslides, heavily eroded stream banks, and stressed trees than there were in my youth. The omens are quite disturbing. I really don't know what can be done about it. The problem is huge. Even though nature is incredibly resilient, I fear the worst.

After breakfast I break camp, knocking the snails off my gear while packing. No hitchhikers! I grab my trekking poles and away I go. It feels good to be back on the trail again. Almost immediately I'm into a short climb. The surrounding forest is boreal – all spruce and fir with a smattering of birch. Not much growing on the forest floor other than moss, ferns, and a hearty member of the lily family called yellow clintonia. A painted trillium pops up – a rare sight this late in the year. Watching for roots and rocks as I walk, I notice moose droppings along with the occasional pile of bear scat. It's early in the day. If I'm quiet enough, perhaps I'll catch a fleeting glimpse of some big furry creature.

I look up every once in a while, keeping my eyes fixed on the yellow blazes of the Kilkenny Ridge Trail. This also happens to be the Cohos Trail even though the government officials who oversee this part of the White Mountain National Forest don't recognize it as such. No CT signs or markers are allowed here. I attribute that to the relative newness of the Cohos Trail, and bureaucratic resistance to change. No doubt this resistance will be overcome in due time.

The Cohos Trail was the brainchild of Kim Robert Nilsen, the author of a book by the same name. He first proposed it in an editorial that appeared in the Lancaster newspaper, *Coos County Democrat*, back in 1978. The trail Nilsen had in mind would traverse the entire length of New Hampshire's largest and northernmost county: Coos. "Cohos" is another spelling of "Coos." Early cartographers used the former term. In 1996, while poring over maps of the Nash Stream Forest and looking for a bushwhacking route north of Sugarloaf Mountain, Nilsen imagined a trail going through there. "I could, " he thought, "Link stretches of existing trail, new paths, old logging roads and woods skidder ways together to form a long-distance trail like the one I proposed so long ago."

In February 1998, Nilsen gathered together enthusiasts for this new trail system. That's how The Cohos Trail Association (TCTA) came into being. Members of the newly formed TCTA set to work right away, putting up CT blazes on existing paths and roads, and cutting new paths where there weren't any. Five years later, a 150-mile trail system was in place, with only 12 more miles left to complete. The CT is now a 170-mile trail, with a few rather long road walks that TCTA hopes to bypass in the near future. The first shelter on the trail, Baldhead Lean-to, was completed in 2003. More would follow. Footbridges have also been built, and some trail work has been undertaken. There is still plenty more work to do, though. The Cohos Trail Association is always looking for volunteers to help finish the task.

I have read about the creation of the Appalachian Trail, Vermont's Long Trail, and other trail systems that I've hiked, but their stories are things of the past, dating back nearly a century, sometimes more. What excites me about The Cohos Trail is that it's brand new – an extensive trail system being created in my lifetime. That's one of the reasons I have wanted to hike it. In a sense, hiking the CT is a venture into the great unknown. It's still a work in progress – not quite ready for the hiking masses, and definitely not for the faint of heart.

While heading downhill, I run into a pair of backpackers from Boston. I stop briefly to trade information with them. Both men are relatively young but look like they've been doing this for a while so I listen carefully to what they have to say. The cabin on Mt. Cabot was crowded last night, and they just came through a lot of downed trees. Their crowded cabin report convinces me that making camp in Bunnell Notch a mile or two short of Mt. Cabot would be the thing to do. I probably won't be able to get any farther than that today, anyhow. As for the downed trees, well, I find myself dealing them soon enough. At one point I have to drop to my knees and crawl beneath one – the brush and blowdown so thick around it that I have no other choice. So it goes.

A tall, slender, solitary hiker comes along shortly after I navigate another particularly dense cluster of downed trees. He doesn't stop to chat. He just smiles and nods his head while passing by. He's traveling light. He's probably one of those 20-miles-a-day hikers that I've often encountered on the Appalachian Trail. While this trail might be a big challenge to me, I'll bet it's just a walk in the woods to him. Looks like he's barely breaking a sweat.

Not too far into my morning hike, I reach an unmarked summit. Presumably this is Middle Weeks, the second of three summits on this ridge, with that bump I crossed an hour ago being South Weeks. Since there are no signs on these summits, I'm not quite sure. I take a short break to drink water then continue hiking. According to my map, I should come to a water source soon.

During a relatively easy downhill stretch, I hear loud voices and barking in the woods behind me. I turn around and see them coming: two very young men and a woman bounding down the trail with two, three, four happy dogs accompanying them. They race towards me, laughing and panting. They're all smiles. No gear to speak of. I step aside as they breeze past. No idea where they came from or where they're going. Does it matter? In his book, *The Practice of the Wild*, Gary Snyder wrote: "Our bodies are wild." Here's proof of that. I envy their exuberance, but mine is a different kind of backcountry happiness. It's enough for me to simply be here, moving ever so slowly through this heavily forested landscape.

Shortly after the parade of joyful hikers and dogs, I encounter a middle-aged man and woman ambling up the trail. They too have a dog. They stop to catch their breath. I stop to converse with them. The black flies are out in full force now and those bloodsucking little beasts are particularly interested in the woman. They swarm around the net covering her head. The man, with his arms, legs and face totally exposed, gets no attention from them at all. A few fly around my head but they prefer hers. It must have something to do with metabolism, or some chemical queue that registers in their tiny insect brains. Who knows? One thing is for certain though: when it comes to bloodsucking bugs, life isn't fair.

In a saddle between two summits I catch something glistening in the dark ribbon of mud cutting through a carpet of moss. That's water to be sure, but is it any good? I step off the trail, going over to find out. Yes sir, this is an excellent water source, so I drop my pack and crouch down next to it. Black flies and mosquitoes have their way with me while I pump but it hardly matters. Goldthread blooms in the green carpet all around me, and there's a delightful smell in the air. What is that smell, anyhow? Rich humus and thriving vegetation… and something I can't quite put my finger on. Ozone perhaps? A needle-like stab at my neck snaps me out of this earthy reverie. I slap the offender into a smear of blood then quickly finish filling my water bottles before returning to the trail.

Another uphill push and I'm over another summit. There are several other water sources along the way. It has been a wet year. I begin the long descent into what I think is Willard Notch but something isn't right. I spot the headwaters of a stream, sure enough, but where is the trail that I'm supposed to cross in this notch? Halfway into another climb, I stop to pee, drink more water and eat lunch. I pull out the mosquito bar and set it up to escape the bugs for a while. Beneath the net, I study my map carefully while munching away at trail mix and crackers laced with peanut butter. I'm not happy about what I discover.

If that was Willard Notch back there, then I should have crossed a trail. I didn't. Have I gone over three summits or only two? That first small rise early this morning could have been a false summit on the shoulder of Mt. Waumbek. Am I halfway up Terrace Mountain or Mt. Weeks? Not sure. There's only one way to find out. I stuff the mosquito bar back into my pack and keep going. With considerable effort, I cross over yet another summit then begin a rather long descent into yet another notch. Paying close attention to my surroundings now, I start thinking the worst. Then I reach the junction with the York Pond Trail. A sign announces it. I'm completely disgusted with myself. How could I have made such a stupid mistake?

It's late afternoon. I came off Mt. Waumbek, over South Weeks, Middle Weeks, and Mt. Weeks, and am now in Willard Notch. I suck down half a liter of water and consume an energy bar while studying my map thoroughly. I still have to get up and over Terrace Mountain before making camp. To make camp now would cost me a day later on. Then this whole trip could unravel. I don't like this assessment, but there it is.

It's an 800-foot climb to the top of Terrace Mountain. There are roughly three miles of trail between here and the stream in Bunnell Notch. Will I make it there before dark? I'm not sure I should even try. I set forth at a measured pace, talking plenty of short breaks along the way. The ascent seems to go on forever. My hips and shoulders hurt. I'm sweating profusely and breathing heavy. My legs start cramping just as I spot what looks like the top. When finally I crest the ridge, I turn my back on a side trail leading to the actual summit of Terrace Mountain then head north. Now it's a race against the sun. I tramp along the ridgeline for a little over an hour before beginning the steep descent into Bunnell Notch. It's a long way down. My knees start complaining. A trail junction sign suddenly appears. What a welcome sight!

The sun has slipped behind the trees but there is still plenty of light to hike by. I turn left onto the Bunnell Notch Trail and follow it until I hear the rush of running water. Then I leave the trail, bushwhacking down to the stream. After finding a somewhat flat spot near the stream, I drop my pack. I have arrived.

4.

Hope it doesn't rain tonight. My camp is not secure. I've strung a line between two conifers then draped my tarp over it, tying off both ends to other conifers. A lazy man's lean-to. This will have to do. The plastic sheet that I use as a ground cloth completely covers the almost flat spot beneath the tarp. I tie the mosquito bar over it and voila! I'm home.

I eat a cold dinner, just like I did last night. It's late. I'm too tired to break out my stove and go through all the rigmarole of cooking and cleaning. Once I'm finished eating, I hang the food bag, brush my teeth then settle into my cozy nest. I have two-thirds of a liter of water left. That'll get me through the night. I'll pump more in the morning. I write in my field journal as long as I can keep my eyes open then quickly fall asleep.

Daybreak. I awaken to the soothing sound of rushing water, and the invigorating smell of the forest on a cool summer morning. Moonshine broke through the trees last night when I got up to relieve myself. These are but a few of the many pleasures of the deep woods. This is why I come out here, time and time again – to groove on the wild. I stumble down to the brook after working some of the stiffness out of my joints and splash its cold, clear water into my face. I let it drip from my beard while gazing at the tiny brook plummeting over rocks. It barely cuts a path through the dense forest understory, ten feet wide at the most. Mountain maple and hobblebush hang from banks thick with moss and downed tree branches. Water falls from one tiny pool to another. Not much to this little stream, yet it is a beautiful thing to behold.

After eating a bowl of granola cereal for breakfast, I study my maps. A big climb up Mt. Cabot this morning, then over another bump in the ridge called The Bulge, then it's downhill all the way to Kilback Pond. A short, gradual climb to Rogers Ledge Tentsite after that. About seven miles altogether. Not far. That's good. I don't think I can handle much more than that today.

So far I seem to be the only hiker out here for the duration, carrying a fully loaded pack through these mountains. In fact, I haven't even seen day hikers or overnight backpackers for a while – not since yesterday morning. Where did they all go? It's Monday morning so the majority of them have probably gone back to work. I'm fortunate enough to still be wandering through these wild woods.

Out here for the duration and carrying a heavy pack. Pretty good for an old guy, I suppose. I recall hiking Vermont's Long Trail back in the 1990s and thinking I was old then. I was 39, a little overweight, and thought the rugged trail was a real challenge. That's laughable now. Today it's a challenge just getting this arthritic body of mine up and running again each morning. I don't have nearly the stamina that I had 24 years ago. It's relative I suppose. What will my hikes be like a decade from now? I can't imagine.

I pump enough water to fill all three bottles, drinking as much as I can in the process. My camp breaks down quickly. Like most seasoned backpackers, I have an efficient packing routine. One last look around after hoisting the load to sore shoulders then I grab my trekking poles and go. It's an easy bushwhack back to the trail.

A little less than 45 pounds. That's what I'm carrying my third day out. Roughly the same weight as when I started, having lost a few pounds of food since then but having filled the third, previously empty liter with water. That's a good trade off, I think.

"Why so heavy?" people often ask me. Well, I'm still carrying six days worth of food for one thing. That's about 10 pounds. Three liters of water is 6 pounds. My old expedition backpack itself weighs over 4 pounds. It has better hip support than the newer, much lighter backpack that I left at home. My first aid kit weighs one and a half pounds, as does my survival kit. During the past forty years, I have used everything in those kits at least once. I also carry a solid-shank hunting knife just in case I get into real trouble out here. There's no better survival tool. There's a little more clothing in my pack than absolutely necessary because I like having plenty of warm, dry clothing to change into when I'm cold and completely soaked to the skin. The elements have cut short several of my outings in the past. Not any more. I'm completely self-reliant and prepared for nearly every contingency. In other words, it's not easy for Mother Nature to shake me loose from the trail once I get on it.

Truth be told, I could slash a few pounds from my load easily enough. I have some old, heavy equipment that should have been replaced with ultra-light gear years ago. Both my water filter and camp stove date back to the 90s. That's kind of silly, I suppose. But if something still works, why replace it? I'm frugal to the extreme. No doubt some backpackers enjoy acquiring the newest latest gear, shaving away those ounces that quickly become pounds, and the expense doesn't matter to them. But that's just not me.

The Bunnell Notch Trail sweeps around the base of Mt. Cabot for half a mile before ending at a T-junction. It's not much of a junction, really. The trail off to the left and going downhill has been closed. No matter. I'm bearing right, headed up Mt. Cabot. I drop my pack long enough to stretch, drink more water and tie a bandana around my forehead in anticipation of a sweaty climb. When I'm ready, I shoulder the pack then stab the ground with my trekking poles while saying: "May the gods of the mountains show mercy!" Then I laugh out loud because they rarely do.

I creep up the mountain steady and slow, remembering a 75-year-old man whom I accompanied up Mt. Pisgah in northern Vermont long ago. I was working as a guide at the time. He looked old and frail. That worried my co-leader and me when we started the hike with him and nine other people. The rest of the group shot up the trail with my co-leader and were soon out of sight. But the old man and I crept along like turtles. We eventually reached the top where everyone else was waiting for us rather impatiently. I was amazed by it, and vowed right then and there that I would ascend Mt. Pisgah when I turn 75. But right now I am facing a 1,200-foot climb up Mt. Cabot with a full pack. This is a different situation, of course. Nonetheless, I keep the same pace as that old man.

This heavily eroded trail – two feet deep in places – has seen a lot of hikers. Not hard to imagine it being a stream during a heavy storm. I haven't seen this much wear and tear since the Starr King ascent two days ago. According to my map, there's a trailhead parking lot only three miles away from here. That explains it.

Halfway up the mountain, I come to a rocky overlook with a great view to the northwest. I see more mountains, of course, and some development in the lowlands peeking from distant hills. Clouds drift through the azure sky overhead. A cool breeze blows from the lowlands, keeping the bugs down as I continue my climb. The gods are showing mercy after all. I stop frequently to catch my breath despite this lucky break. Soon I am anticipating the top, thinking it's just beyond the next rise. But that's just wishful thinking. "It'll be what it'll be," I declare rather stoically. Then I keep going.

There is no dishonest way to climb a mountain – the help of a Sherpa notwithstanding. I contemplate this while putting one foot in front of another. It feels almost righteous to do so. With all the deceit there is in the world these days – all the false advertising, misinformation and lies about how much easier our lives could be – it's good to get away and just sweat for a day or so while pressing steadily uphill. A good climb is spiritually cleansing. One grunts, pants, and sweats out the lies, thus gaining a much-needed perspective on things.

The trail crests soon enough. Cabot Cabin comes into view. I drop my pack then go inside to look around. The exterior of the old cabin, with shingled siding and lots of windows, has a certain charm to it. But the interior is beat. Trash, a dirty floor, discolored walls, cracked window glass, and worn bunks. It's a good place to get out of the weather. That is all. I can only imagine the use it gets. I go back outside to enjoy the fresh mountain air and rest a bit while writing in my journal.

A lone hiker comes along while I'm writing. I greet him with a big smile and a friendly hello. He's a silver-haired fellow about my age – thinner and in better shape than me, I'd say. His name is Tim. He's out for one day only, even though his pack is nearly half the size of mine. I mistook him for an overnight hiker. He has everything he needs to spend a night in the woods, he tells me, if it comes to that. Tim is prepared. "Yeah, it's like that when you hike alone enough," I respond. Tim whips out his cell phone and makes a quick call to his wife to let her know that he's on top and okay. He tells me that a 69-year-old man died on the Kilkenny Ridge Trail just a few days ago. A woman died on Mt. Washington the day before that.

So he's playing it as safe as anyone can play it while still hiking alone.

Tim tells me that he's 67 years old. I tell him I'm only four years younger. We agree that it isn't the smartest thing for either one of us to be out here hiking alone. "But these mountains would be a good place to die," Tim says. I can't argue with that. Still I strongly believe a rigorous hike is life affirming, especially when I do it alone. As prepared as I may be, I come out here to live my life, not die. Tim agrees with me on that count, as well.

Tim recently acquired a "hike safe" card from the New Hampshire Fish and Game Department. "It's not expensive," he says. With that he is not liable for the costs of being rescued, if it comes to that. I grumble, not happy at all about the advent of hiker's insurance. He adds that the State usually doesn't charge for rescues unless the hiker in question has done something negligent. I can't help but laugh. "Some people would consider it negligent for a sixty-something to be hiking alone through country like this," I say. Tim smiles. In that regard, we are both guilty as charged, though mine is the clearly the greater offense.

I'm ready to head out the same time that Tim is so we hike together to the actual summit of Mt. Cabot. It's another 200 feet up and half a mile away. As we are walking, Tim informs me that he's a retired newspaperman living in Rhode Island. I tell him I'm a combination writer/bookseller, and that I live in Vermont but grew up in Ohio. I occasionally go back to Ohio to visit my mother who is dying. Correction: she died two months ago. Tim says both his parents are gone now. He focuses on his grandchildren these days. "Grandchildren are a true joy, aren't they?" I say. "They are," Tim responds. Young people are just beginning to explore the world and that's a wonderful thing to behold, even as older generations pass away. Life goes on. The planet doesn't stop turning. People continue going about their business. As difficult as it is to accept when a loved one dies, life goes on.

Because we are busy talking, the final ascent seems effortless. Upon reaching a sign marking the wooded summit, I use Tim's phone to snap a picture of him. Then he uses my camera to snap one of me. A mother/daughter pair of day hikers reach the summit shortly after we do, so I offer to take pictures of them with their phones, as well. While I'm doing that, Tim slips away, going back the same way he came. I head north, descending Mr. Cabot on the trail to The Bulge and beyond. Interactions with other hikers are often cut short that way. Tim and I hit it off, but now we are both hiking alone again. Just like that.

5.

Midday. I'm on top of The Bulge, 3,950 feet above sea level – just a couple hundred feet lower than Mt. Cabot. This is the last of eight summits on the Kilkenny Ridge and I'm glad to be done with it all. Now comes a long descent to Unknown Pond, and another to Kilback Pond. I count the 100-foot contour lines on my map while forcing down an energy bar and some nuts to keep up my strength. There are fifteen of them.

      The trail beyond The Bulge is steep and rocky. My knees complain right away. The footing is bad in a lot of places so it's hard on my ankles as well. When I was in my 20s, I used to rock-hop down mountains effortlessly. Not any more. In my so-called golden years now, downhill is almost as difficult as uphill. It's a different kind of difficulty, of course. Going uphill is all about aerobics, muscles and stamina. When going downhill, the joints are the issue. After forty years of doing this, mine are wearing out. Thank god for sturdy trekking poles! I lean into them with every step.

Without them, I couldn't do this descent – not with a full pack tugging at my shoulders.

I pass a side trail leading to the summit of The Horn. Then the fun really begins. Lots of boulders and an even steeper descent. I take my time with it, humming and whistling down the mountain as if this is no big deal at all. Then my right ankle rolls, reminding me that I could still stumble and fall even with trekking poles firmly in hand. So I cut my pace to a crawl.

Once I'm past the steepest part of the descent, I start looking for Unknown Pond. My anticipation of it is a bit premature, though. The trail dips down to a rivulet in a crease before rising fifty feet or so. I stop to check my map, waving away black flies in the process. Okay, the pond is just a little farther ahead. Keep going.

I catch a glimpse of still, blue water through the trees. Soon I reach an opening where the ground eases to a shallow inlet. Not a good place to pump water so I keep going. It's a short walk around Unknown Pond to the camping area. Just before reaching it, I spot a small, rocky beach. Yeah, that'll do quite nicely. I step out of the trees then slide the heavy pack off my shoulders and lean it against a bush. Out comes the water filter, along with all three water bottles. I crouch at the water's edge and set to work.

Dragonflies and damselflies patrol the surface of the pond while I pump. They take their fill of unsuspecting mosquitoes and flies, keeping the rest away. Ah, if only I could train one of these ancient-looking, winged beasts to follow me around all day. Then my hikes would be bug free. They glisten in the sunlight as they fly past. Sunlight shimmers off the slightly rippled surface of the pond, as well. A wall of dark conifers wraps around it. Beyond the trees, The Horn rises abruptly into the blue sky. Hard to believe I was up there a little more than an hour ago.

About a hundred yards away, a solitary camper appears along the edge of the pond. He squats down and does something – I can't make out what. He's in some kind of zone, no doubt aware of my presence but not acknowledging it. Too absorbed in the moment. This incredibly quiet, peaceful pond has worked its magic on the man. I see myself in him, recalling a pond in the Adirondacks where I hung out for days while doing a lot of nothing. But mine is a different mindset right now. I'm on the move. That is, I will be as soon as I finish pumping water. Two bottles full, one more to go. I stop and drink some water while looking around. Hoo-boy! This place is enchanting... Hard to stay focused on the task at hand.

On the pond's surface, not three feet away, a caddis fly slowly beats its wings dry before taking off. It just emerged from the water. Another caddis fly is already airborne. If I had my fly rod with me, I could be plying these waters for brook trout. They must be here. Are they feeding on these caddis flies yet? Doesn't look like it. Perhaps they are doing so beneath the surface. Much of what goes on in the natural world escapes the eye, even when one is looking.

A newt swims through the transparent water at my feet, barely visible against the muddy bottom. A bullfrog croaks somewhere off to the right. Is that a hawk soaring overhead or some other kind of raptor? There sure is a lot going on here. Maybe I should stay. But no, I need to do a couple more miles before calling it a day.

I cap the third bottle once it is full then pack up and go. It's a short walk around the pond, retracing my steps. Then I'm back on the Kilkenny Ridge Trail. The haze in my head clears as I pick up my pace, crossing over a knoll. My blood is up again and the black flies know it. They follow me as the trail eases downhill. Heaven forbid that I should go anywhere without them.

Now it's a long, steady descent through thickets of hobblebush, brakes and ferns, with a few brambles thrown in for good measure. Moving out of the shadows, I pass through sunny gaps in the trees where the understory encroaches upon the trail. I catch a glimpse of Rogers Ledge in the distance – a great mound of exposed rock rising from a sea of green. It looks far away. In the darker places beneath conifers bunchberry, starflower and a few trilliums are still in bloom. When at last the ground levels out, it becomes boggy.   A long stretch of puncheon crosses a particularly wet spot.   Can't imagine trying to get around or through it without this narrow, wooden walkway underfoot.   Whoa!   This is mosquito country! They're all over me in no time.   Kilback Pond materializes out of this saturated landscape and I'm happy to see it.   But I don't stop any longer than it takes to drink a little water.   I'll rest later.   Rogers Ledge Tentsite, my destination, isn't far away.

While crossing a stream a short while later, I wonder if perhaps I should stop and top off my water bottles before finishing today's hike.   The mosquitoes and black flies urge me to keep going.   Soon enough I spot a sign pointing to the right.   A side trail takes me to Rogers Ledge Tentsite.   It's a sweet piece of flat, open ground beneath birches and maples.   There's a privy nearby, but no water source here.   Tomorrow morning I'll have to backtrack to that stream that I just crossed in order to fill my bottles.   Hmm…

Late afternoon.   There are still several hours of daylight left, but I waste no time making camp.   I string a line between two birches then stretch my tarp over it, anchoring the guy lines in firm, dry ground.   The result is a roomy tent-like structure with the mosquito bar underneath.   Next I throw a line over the high branch of another birch tree for my food bag.   Then I hang my sweaty clothes on the long empty line stretching between my tarp and one of the birches.   Think I'll hold off cooking dinner until the temperature drops a bit. The bugs won't be so bad then. To temporarily escape them, I slip beneath the netting to study my maps and rest for a while.

End of the third day and I am incredibly sore. Along with the usual aching joints and muscles, an old rib injury has come back to haunt me. The Kilkenny Ridge Trail is kicking my ass. Long day tomorrow, starting with a short climb up Roger's Ledge first thing in the morning. Then it's all downhill until I reach South Pond. Including the access road from South Pond to Highway 110, it's a three-mile road walk to Nash Stream Forest. After that there will be another climb into a notch and a couple more miles of trail before I reach Devil's Rest Shelter. Eleven miles altogether. Another long day, like yesterday. Seems like I'm pushing my body to its limits. Perhaps I should rethink this hike. It might be wise to finish at Dixville Notch, as originally planned, instead of going all the way to Pittsburg. That's something to consider, anyhow.

Dinnertime. While lifting the netting and rolling away from it, I notice a tear in its seam. I dig a small roll of duct tape out of my pack and temporarily repair the tear, thinking I'll do a more thorough job later when I get home. Then again, maybe I should retire the mosquito bar and the tarp with it. Maybe it's time to rethink how I camp, as well as how far I hike on any given outing. A single-person tent would be so much easier to set up. Ah, but I like the openness of a tarp. I like being in the woods instead of inside a tent. All the same, it might be time to start doing things differently.

A chicken and rice dehydrated meal for dinner this evening. The camp stove fires up effortlessly and water is boiling in no time. I pour the steaming water into a pouch full of freeze-dried food then wait a long ten minutes. When dinner is ready I gobble it all down. I haven't been very hungry lately but this tastes great. And it improves my mood considerably. Afterward I sit and sip lemonade and think. But I'm a little too tired to think about anything more than my basic physical needs. The trail has reduced me to my animal self. That's not a bad thing, I suppose.

I'm back under the tarp shortly after dinner. I write in my journal for a while. Down for the count before daylight fades away. Saw plenty of moose tracks and pellets around Kilback Pond this afternoon. Moose hang out there, obviously. Wouldn't be too surprised if one wanders into my camp tonight. That would be something. Keep my headlamp handy just in case. Haven't seen any moose on this trip yet. Haven't seen moose in years. Long overdue.

6.

I awaken to the sound of mosquitoes buzzing on the other side of the net. The air is still. Temps cooled overnight but are warming up fast. Thought I heard moose clomping along the trail last night. Now that I'm fully awake, I'm not so sure. No moose came into the tenting area. Still there's a good chance I'll encounter one on the trail this morning. After all it's early and I'll be on the move soon. Have to get going. Long day ahead.

The melodic, flute-like song of a wood thrush fills the air as I roll away from my comfy nest beneath the tarp. How I love that song! It lifts my spirits, energizing me. It assures me that I'm right where I belong, deep in a wild forest. I drop the food bag dangling from a nearby birch then immediately start breaking camp. I'm down to three-quarters of a liter of water and the next water source is on the other side of Rogers Ledge. I could backtrack to the stream a quarter mile away but don't want to take the time to do that.

I'll get water and eat breakfast later. Just break camp and go.

Shortly after leaving Rogers Ledge Tentsite, I flush a grouse hen from the understory. She immediately goes into her time-tested ruse, pretending to have a broken wing and calling out in distress to draw me away from her nearby nest of chicks. I feel the ancient predator in me responding to it. Her cleverness, my gut reaction. The difference between intelligence and instinct is not as obvious as we brainy hominids like to think it is.

The short, steep climb up Rogers Ledge is relatively easy, thanks to strategically placed stones. Thank you trail workers, whoever you are! The sudden appearance of improved trail deep in the woods never ceases to amaze me. Someone had to hike here and toil for a day just to make my passing through a little easier. I stop a few times during the climb to catch my breath. Then I'm on top.

Rogers Ledge is only three thousand feet above sea level, but it stands apart from the cluster of mountains on Kilkenny Ridge to the south so there's a commanding view from its summit. Wild country spreads away from it in all directions. I drop my backpack against a large rock then walk out to the cliff's edge. To the southwest Mt. Cabot, The Bulge and the Horn peek above the heavily forested slope rising towards them. The tent site where I camped last night is somewhere in the valley below, not far away. Off to the left, the Presidential Range looms on the southeastern horizon. And to the east, steam rises from the wood chip plant that powers the city of Berlin, nestled in a distant valley. A magnificent, wild world stretched out beneath an overcast sky. Silence broken only by a few songbirds in the distance. And me in the middle of it all. This is why I still pound the trail even though I'm sixty-three years old. Not just for the view, but to stand alone in the middle of a sprawling forest and feel the freedom of the hills surge through my aching body. I love going wild, if only for a week or so at a time.

I sit down long enough to eat an energy bar and suck down half a liter of water while studying my topo map. Then I shoulder the forty-pound load and go. Day four on the Cohos Trail. I still have a long hike ahead of me: exiting the White Mountains, doing a three-mile road walk, then venturing several more miles farther north into the Nash Stream Forest before reaching Devil's Rest Shelter. I have to reach that shelter today in order to have any chance of going all the way to Pittsburg during the time remaining. All the way to Pittsburg, hmm… That was the plan when I started this hike, but now I'm thinking it might have to be amended. Pittsburg is still sixty miles away. My body is wearing out faster than expected. I need to be smart about this. I need to think differently. I don't have the stamina of the young man who started backpacking in earnest forty years ago. And the passage of time has left its mark on my knees and other joints.

The trail easing down from Rogers Ledge is delightful – a nearly effortless walk along a narrow earthen path cutting through the vibrant green understory. Lady slippers, yellow clintonia, trilliums and other spring wildflowers are still in bloom even though it's June. A cool breeze is blowing now, keeping the bugs down. A wood thrush sings nearby. My sturdy hiking poles click against the occasional root or rock as I amble along, well aware how fortunate I am to be here. The surrounding landscape is so incredibly beautiful! As late as April I wasn't sure this trip was going to happen. My mother's health was deteriorating fast so I thought I might be making yet another impromptu drive back to Ohio to see her this summer instead of going for a hike. But she died so here I am, on the trail and happy.

I stop, leaning into my trekking poles as the image of my frail, old mother flashes through my head. She's gone. She really is gone, isn't she? Parkinson's disease finally confounded her. A quick trip back to Ohio in the end of April confirmed that. After several years of steady decline, my mother is dead. I burst into tears, dropping to my knees as the searing reality of it strikes with full force. The woman who raised me, who has been in my life for as long as I can remember, no longer exists. I cling to my hiking poles while bent over heaving – a heavy pack still tugging at my shoulders. There's no one around so I don't hold back. I cry for what seems like hours, head bowed and tears running down my cheeks. I let it all out. Then I collect myself, slowly rising to my feet. I use a sweat-soaked bandana to wipe away the tears before continuing my hike, focusing on the trail ahead. I still have a long way to go today.

A mile downhill from Rogers Ledge, the trail becomes all roots and rocks. Young spruce trees competing for light crowd the sketchy path. Their boughs brush hard against my arms as I plow through them. The cool breeze that kept the bugs away earlier has died away. When suddenly I feel the sharp stab of pain in my forearm, I reach over to swat the large bug causing it, knocking myself off balance in the process. Down I go, twisting my right ankle in the rocks. The sheer size of the bloody crater in my arm is surprising. Was that a deer fly? Probably. But it's no big deal, I tell myself. Just a bug bite. So I get up and keep going. All the same, my right ankle throbs while I push through the spruce.

After drinking the last of my water, I start thinking about getting more. The headwaters of Cold Stream aren't far away. I can just barely hear the faint yet unmistakable sound of water rushing in the distance. Soon I am stepping over seeps and rivulets merging into each other. A tiny stream appears. I start looking for a good place to pump water and spot one not far from the trail. I drop my pack and bushwhack over to it with three empty bottles and a water filter in hand. Pumping water is a pleasant break from hiking despite the bugs swarming around my head. I'm crouched next to the stream and grooving on the wildness all around me. Water breaking over rocks has a soothing affect, washing away some of the sting of my mother's death. The sight and sound of it mesmerizes me. I gulp down half a liter of water while pumping. Once all three of my bottles are full, I return to the trail to resume my walk.

Cold Stream widens and becomes more animated as I make my way towards South Pond. The beaten path underfoot also widens. A large body of water emerges from the trees and suddenly the shoreline trail underfoot looks strangely familiar. I was here four years ago, on a scouting trip for this trek, hiking this section of trail with my longhaired German shepherd dog, Matika. But Matika isn't hiking with me any more. Like my mother, Matika is also gone. I miss her. For a dozen years, that happy dog was by my side during nearly all my ventures into the wild. Now I hike alone.

A solitary loon greets me with its exuberant call as I approach the South Pond Recreation Area. I pass a patch of forget-me-nots that remind me of Judy. That's her favorite flower. Now I'm missing her, as well. Whoa! All this loss and longing for others – it's a bit much. It confuses me emotionally, infusing my hiking happiness with sadness.

A large sandy beach comes into view. The trail gives way to a grassy area full of picnic tables behind a meticulously groomed beach. Tiger swallowtail butterflies flutter over the grass. All of a sudden the shadowy wildness of the forest has become a tidy, open, recreation area. I drop my pack on the bench seat of a picnic table shaded by a copse of small maple trees. I look around. A robin hopping across the grass belts out its joyous song. An American flag flaps in the wind from a pole nearby, but there's no park ranger in sight. I step into the changing building nearby only to find it empty. It's late morning, almost noon, on a beautiful summer day, but I'm the only one here. How odd.

7.

While sitting at the picnic table, I slather bug dope onto my face, neck and arms so that I can eat lunch in peace. Then I open my pack and prepare a simple meal: trail mix, sesame seeds, a granola bar, and lemonade powder stirred into a cup of water. Suddenly two twenty-something women appear with a young girl and even younger boy in tow. They are carrying a cooler, beach towels and water toys. The boy spots me right away and waves. I wave back. They park themselves on the beach, a few feet from the water's edge and forty yards away from me. Another young woman and child appear shortly thereafter. They too find a place for themselves on the sand. Now the South Pond Recreation Area is occupied by those who aren't just passing through. Curiously enough, the bugs aren't bothering any of them.

I'm not that hungry. I'm half-sick from exhaustion and grief. I choke down some food so that I have enough strength to keep going. I drink all the lemonade, along with nearly a liter of water. I pull out my map to see what lies ahead. There are seven miles left to do today. After walking the park access road out to highway 110 and up Percy Road to the trailhead, it'll be a steady climb into Bald Mountain Notch before doing a long, relatively easy descent to Devil's Rest Shelter. There's nowhere to legally camp between here and there. Not that it matters. I have to reach Devil's Rest Shelter today in order to reach Pittsburg in the days remaining. Oh sure, I can do the distance to that shelter, but there won't be much left of me afterward. I'll have to take a zero day tomorrow – a day to rest before continuing farther north. I had planned on taking a zero day at Old Hermit Shelter the day after tomorrow, but I don't think my body can handle another day of trail pounding. The summits of the Kilkenny Ridge Trail have wiped me out. My body is telling me that I need a break. None of my hip, knee or ankle joints are happy. Truth is, going all the way to Pittsburg might be out of the question no matter when I take a zero day. And with that rather depressing thought, I pack up my things and go.

My trekking poles click against asphalt as I amble along the park access road. I pass two female rangers at the park entrance. They are deeply engaged in conversation. They greet me with curt hellos, perfunctory nods and smiles before continuing their talk. A pickup truck drives by, then a car. The mile and a half walk out to the highway goes quickly. Soon I am meandering along the shoulder of the highway as cars and trucks roar past. A few steps over a bridge across the Upper Ammonoosuc River, then I turn onto Percy Road. The road is easy enough to walk, but the hard surface underfoot pounds my tender feet until I feel a couple hot spots. Upon reaching the trailhead to Nash Stream Forest, I drop my pack and take off my boots to inspect my feet. Sure enough, I have a few blisters. They are long overdue, actually. I set to work patching them with band-aids and moleskin.

The Nash Stream Forest is the beginning of the Great North Woods. Having departed the White Mountain National Forest, I am now entering the upper half of Coos County where there are more moose, bear and other wild animals than people. Resorts and logging operations are prevalent in this region, and most of the land is privately owned. The Nash Stream Forest Natural Area is the exception to the rule, owned by the State and managed by the New Hampshire Division of Forests and Lands. Recreation is encouraged and a dirt road cutting into the 40,000-acre Nash Stream watershed provides easy access. But no camping was allowed here until recently, making it tricky for hikers like me to pass through. Fortunately, the State has allowed The Cohos Trail Association to establish a couple campsites along the trail to accommodate hikers.

"In a very real sense, the Nash Stream Forest is the heart of the Cohos Trail," Kim Robert Nilsen wrote in his book *The Cohos Trail*. This wild forest lies halfway between the northern and southern ends of the CT, and the pathway traversing it is the least developed. Here yellow blazes and the twin-peak CT trail signs, fashioned after the Percy Peaks located in the middle of Nash Stream Forest, stitch together the snowmobile paths, abandoned logging roads, old trails and newly cut ones that wind through this very rugged, beautiful country. The makeshift nature of this pathway is exactly what the Cohos Trail is all about.

After patching my feet, I shoulder my pack and follow the bright yellow CT trail markers up a pleasant woods road carpeted with Canada mayflower. A mile into the woods, I reach a wooden snowmobile bridge spanning a stream. This seems like a good place to top off my water bottles so that's what I do.

Once I'm moving again, the woods road turns to the west while the CT trail markers veer away sharply to the northwest. Good thing I was paying attention. Had I been daydreaming, I would have missed it. I follow the markers up the narrowing trail as it steadily climbs into Bald Mountain Notch. I stop several times to catch my breath along the way. The path underfoot becomes less and less distinct. The notch itself is thick with vegetation, bug-ridden and boggy. There is very little in the way of puncheon or any other trail work beneath my feet. More often than not, I find myself ankle deep in mud. Not easy traveling. I'm *really* tired now, but still have miles to go before I can call it a day.

On the other side of the notch, the going gets better as the trail widens into a woods road. Then the CT blazes veer off to the right again, as if easy-to-follow woods roads should be avoided at all costs. I follow the bright yellow blazes along a fairly new section of trail called the Rowells Link. It's slow going to say the least – all roots, rocks and mud holes. Or is fatigue warping my perception on things? I swat a black fly while stumbling along, then my right ankle turns and down I go. Fortunately the boggy, rain-soaked ground softens the impact. I get up, brush myself off and keep going. A brand new footbridge suddenly appears in the middle of nowhere – unexpected and somewhat out of context with the rest of the Rowells Link Trail. It spans Rowells Brook. Someone has been doing some serious trail work out here. I cross it with ease before continuing my slog. Eventually, Rowells Link empties into a woods road. I follow it to a junction with yet another woods road. This one goes down to the Devil's Rest Shelter. I hobble along it for half a mile, until a sign points down a side trail to an unseen shelter. A one-minute walk along this side trail then I drop my pack on the shelter floor with a great big sigh of relief. Made it! Eleven and a half miles today.

Devil's Rest Shelter sits on a piece of conservation land called the Kauffmann Forest that adjoins the Nash Stream Forest. Technically speaking, this shelter is half a mile off the Cohos Trail. The Cohos Trail Association built it last year with the help of Garland Mill Timberframes. The shelter still smells of freshly milled wood. There's a picture on the wall of the twenty volunteers who constructed it. There's a compost toilet nearby and plenty of benches scattered around the shelter, but no campfire ring. Fires aren't allowed here.

I tie up my mosquito bar in a corner of the shelter. Then I sling a line in the trees for my food bag. I'm dog-tired so the latter task takes more time and effort than it usually does. Once that's done, I slip beneath the netting. In another hour or so, once the air temperature cools down enough to ground the black flies, I'll fix dinner – the same tactic used yesterday. I'd like to get something hot in my belly, but right now I'm happy enough just lying on the hard floor of the shelter, sprawled out and bug-free.

My joints are weakening faster than expected and I'm running out of steam. Hiking all the way to Pittsburg is looking less and less likely. I'll be lucky to make it to Dixville Notch. Can't help but wonder what's wrong with me, why I'm having such a hard time on this trek. Just don't have the stamina that I used to have. The 100-Mile Wilderness in northern Maine was tough enough when I hiked it ten years ago, but nothing like this. Last year's 46-mile trek on the AT with my old hiking buddy John took a lot out of me, but at least I was still moving on day five. That won't be the case this time. Tomorrow has to be a zero day.

Late evening, with less than an hour of daylight left, I pull out my stove and boil up water for ramen noodles and tea. The noodles hit the spot. I eat all of them even though I'm not that hungry. There's a rumbling in my gut right now. Not a good sign. This is my third dry camp and I'm more than just a little concerned about the consequences of that. My hygiene hasn't been the best on this trip. I'm feeling grungy, and grunge eventually takes a toll out here.

I clean the cooking pot, sling my food bag back into the trees then brush my teeth in the long summer twilight. A chipmunk chatters, a woodpecker knocks, a wood thrush sings. I check out a couple lady's slippers growing close to the shelter but don't have enough energy to snoop around much more than that. A loon calls in the distance. It's probably on Christine Lake, not more than half a mile away as the crow flies. I sit on the edge of the shelter for a while, wondering what I'll do while hanging out here tomorrow. Whatever. Figure that out in the morning. Underneath the net a short while later, I write in my journal by headlamp. Then I'm down for the count as darkness overtakes the forest.

8.

I slowly awaken to the songs of birds and the roar of truck traffic. The trucks sound like they're only a hundred yards away, yet all I see is forest when I open my eyes. This confuses my half-asleep brain. Can't be in both the wild and the developed lowlands at the same time. Highway 110 is a couple miles south of this shelter, I recall from my last map reading. And sound travels far through the silent forest.

First clear thought of the day: I could push all the way to Pittsburg if I want to, but that would completely drain me. Is it worth it? Of course not. No one cares how far I hike. I certainly don't care. Mileage? That's not why I came out here. What then is this outing all about? To immerse my self in the wild and groove on nature, that's what. So why not take a couple zero days? How long before my food runs out and I have to return to the developed lowlands? Why not take *three* zero days – one at each shelter between here and Dixville Notch, hopscotching along the trail? Now there's an idea.

Credit where credit is due: my primary care physician is the one who suggested that I take two zero days. That was back in January, during my annual check-up. I remember smiling at the notion, then completely dismissing it. She's not a hiker, I kept thinking, so she doesn't understand. But what is there to understand? I come out here to groove on nature. The rigor of the trail is only a means to this end. I don't judge those who want to push themselves, seeing how far they can go. I too enjoy hiking hard every once in a while. But that's not what I'm all about.

I remember passing a beautiful pond while I was hiking the 100-Mile Wilderness ten years ago, thinking how nice it would be to just hang out there for a week. That's pretty much what I did at Pillsbury Lake in the Adirondacks, back in 2017. But I grew a restless while I was there, and became too deeply immersed in my thoughts to fully enjoy being in the moment. It's not easy striking the right balance between movement and staying put, or between being in the moment and reflection. And the right mix varies from person to person, no doubt. Perhaps it's time for me to try a different approach.

Just now a wood thrush sings its beautiful, intoxicating, flute-like song. I have always loved that song. I hear something mystical in it. "Whenever a man hears it," Henry David Thoreau once wrote, "He is young, and Nature is in her spring. Wherever he hears it, it is a new world and a free country, and the gates of heaven are not shut against him." My sentiments exactly, though I'm no longer young by any measure. Young at heart, perhaps. The wood thrush's song reminds me that there is more to nature than meets the eye, and that heaven is here/now. That seems like a strange thing to think while lying on the floor of a shelter called Devil's Rest. Hell is here too, I suppose. After all, hell is suffering and life has plenty of that, as well.

Loss. I suffer the most from a sense of loss. I've lost a good number of family members and friends over the years, and there's more to come I'm sure. My 90-year-old father is teetering on the edge of the precipice even as I lie here. A couple months ago I lost my mother. Right before her death, I lost my canine companion, Matika. A few years ago I lost a boyhood friend, Jeff, who was born on the same day I was. That made me acutely aware of my own mortality. Yet life goes on, as the wood thrush reminds me. Despite all loss, those of us still alive keep on living.

A siren wails in the distance. It grows louder then fades away. Someone is in trouble. Perhaps that person is reaching the end of his or her life. I think of my mother and how she lived her life as fully as she could, right up to the end. Her body wore out slowly,

bit by bit. How frail she looked the last time I saw her!
I recall seeing my old boss and good friend David right
before he died. He too was reduced to skin and bones.
The body of each and every one of us deteriorates.
Then it shuts down. The aging process often comes as
something of a shock. Life doesn't last as long as we
think it will. The earth turns, the days go by, and all too
soon we are old men and women. Then we die. All
living things die – that is nature's way. No matter how
many trees there are standing in a forest, in due time
every one of them will eventually hit the ground. And
new ones come along to replace them. No one disputes
this, yet it doesn't seem quite right. We long for
immortality, for *something* to be immortal anyhow.

      Well, I didn't come out here to brood about life
and death. My mother certainly wouldn't have
approved. I may be getting older but I'm still alive, still
interested in being in the world. The trail's end will
come soon enough. No sense dwelling on it. Best to
simply make the most of the journey. So with that in
mind, I think I'll take as many zero days as I need to
take in order to enjoy the rest of this outing.

Rising from my comfy nest on the shelter floor, I use
the last of the water on hand to fix tea for breakfast.
Immediately following breakfast, I pull on my boots
and walk a quarter mile down the woods road to the
nearest brook to refill my water bottles. I drink half a

liter of the cold, clear stream water in the process. Once the bottles are full, I rinse out my bandanas and a particularly stinky t-shirt. Looks like it's going to be another beautiful day in the forest. I collect all my things then walk back to the shelter to hang out for the day.

With a sleeping pad as a seat and a rolled up sleeping bag providing lumbar support, I prop myself against the shelter wall and start writing in my journal. Just then a hummingbird suddenly appears, suspended in mid-air right in front of my face, taking me completely by surprise. For a split second I see it as a giant mosquito. Then I laugh, realizing my mistake. And the hummingbird is gone – just like that. It's more like a hallucination than an encounter.

A solitary hiker pops up next. Fortunately, he's moving much slower than the hummingbird. We exchange greetings then converse for a bit. His name is Karl. He's a fellow about my age who comes out here to recharge his batteries. He's in the process of hiking all of the AMC trails in New Hampshire. Today he's hiking up the Percy Peaks. Started at the nearby Christine Lake. Like me, he avoids the busy trails of the Presidential Range, preferring to hike alone, off the beaten path. I tell him I'm hiking the Cohos Trail, taking a zero day before continuing to Dixville Notch. Saying it out loud makes this change of plans real. Karl wishes me the best of luck then takes off. I return to my journaling.

"Life goes on, though we cannot account for it," John Burroughs wrote in *Accepting the Universe*. He was an old man by then and had experienced plenty of loss. But life goes on. Every day people are born while others die. All living things come and go. Human beings are no exception to this, yet we are self-aware enough to be horrified by it. Love is forever, yet the people we love die. Why doesn't the world stop turning when they do? Life goes on… as if the ones we love are not critical to existence of the world at large. It doesn't seem right. It seems like an affront to love itself. Because of this we are faced with a hard choice: either we allow ourselves to be paralyzed by the death of a loved one, or we get on with the business of living. It's not much of a choice, really. Eventually we have to get on with the business of living.

Gone but not forgotten. I carry with me a few items that remind me of loved ones. The tent poles I use to set up my tarp are left over from a cheap tent that my friend Jeff gave me years before he passed. I purchased my mosquito bar from Jerry's Army Navy store when I was working for him. Both the store and Jerry are gone now. During the colder months, I wear a heavy watch cap that my grandmother gave me one Christmas. She passed away in the 1990s. Has it really been twenty-five years? For just as long I have carried in my back pocket the Swiss army knife that my mother gave me. I have a few items with me from the living, as well: Judy's sleeping pad that I'm sitting on, a hunting knife and an old backpack purchased from friends long ago, and so on. Truth is, I'm never completely alone when I hike. I'm never without something that reminds me of a loved one.

Fifth day on the trail and I'm missing Judy. The older I get, the harder it is to be away from her more than a few days at a time. This is natural, I suppose. Thank god I married the right woman! Judy knows that I need to come out here alone every once in a while, for a week or more at a time, and she enjoys her own company when I'm gone. That said I don't like being away from her, especially when I'm grieving. But that's the price I am paying this time around for a little deep woods solitude. The arrangement is only temporary, I keep telling myself.

Midday. I spot a tick crawling across the top of my mosquito bar. Without giving the matter a second thought, I kill it. Forget about bears – what nearly everyone mentions whenever I start talking about my wilderness excursions. The real threats out here are giardia and ticks. Giardia is a water-borne parasite that can wreak havoc on one's digestive system. That's why purifying water is so important. Ticks can do much worse. Some of them carry Lyme disease, which can make the rest of one's life miserable. And with that thought I rub some Deet onto my exposed skin. Although I suspect there's something evil lurking in a chemical called *diethyltoluamide*, I'm sure that using it is better than the alternative.

Late afternoon. I awaken from a long nap feeling worse than I did when I went down. My stomach is gurgling. Hmm… loose bowels. Bacteria, exhaustion, or something worse? Hard to say. Don't want to think about it too much, though. No sense jumping to conclusions. See how I feel tomorrow.

Once I'm fully awake, I discover a second tick crawling up my pants legs. I kill it then slather on more bug dope. I slip into something of a funk in the process. The last thing I need right now is to find one of those little buggers embedded in me. Wonder when I picked them up, and how many more I've brought with me into this shelter. That's assuming, of course, that they weren't already here.

The sun has given way to clouds. A few raindrops are falling. I waste no time retrieving my drying t-shirt and bandanas from the clothesline that I've strung between trees. Shortly thereafter, a steady rain commences. It drums against the metal shelter roof, making me glad to be under cover. Water starts dripping from the roof edge. The bugs suddenly disappear. I bide my time, doing a little first aid on myself: triple antibiotic salve to a couple cuts on my arm, powder to rashes, and new patches to the blisters on my feet in anticipation of tomorrow's hike. Then I pull out my journal and jot down a life-affirming things to do list – things like trout fishing, writing poetry and being with loved ones. Things that make life worth living. It seems like a good way to spend the rest of a rainy afternoon.

9.

A heavy rain falls right before dusk, right after I've pumped water down by the stream. Three liters secured this evening so I won't have to pump in the morning. During the break in the rain, I also managed to fix dinner, clean up and sling my food bag back into the trees. Good timing. Now all I have to do is run out for a final pee before settling in for the night. I strip off my t-shirt before doing that, just to keep it dry. Then I'm back in the shelter with all my dry gear, listening to the rumble of thunder in the distance. A bona fide summer storm is underway.

I bed down early in anticipation of getting up early. Big hike tomorrow, up to the col between the Percy Peaks then north to Old Hermit Shelter. About ten miles. No big climbs after the Percys but the trail will be challenging enough, I'm sure. Comparing my old CT trail map to the updated one, I notice a three-mile reroute called the Trio Trail. It stays away from the dirt road that cuts through the Nash Stream Forest.

Got a feeling it'll be rough going along that section of trail. No matter. If I get a decent night's sleep, it won't be a problem.

Thursday morning. Sixth day on the trail. I awaken to the sound of water dripping through the trees. I don't think it's raining right now but the forest is completely soaked. It rained off and on all night. The soothing sound of rainfall made it easy to sleep, which I did for nearly ten hours. Now I am well rested and ready to hike. But breakfast first. After retrieving my food bag from the trees, I break out my stove. Then I boil up water for tea. There's a little water in the bottom of the food bag, but no food lost as a result. The heavy, trash compactor bag inside the food bag provided extra protection. Oh yeah, this old Boy Scout thinks of everything.

After breakfast I waste no time packing up my gear. I do a little stretching to loosen my tight muscles before shouldering the backpack, then I am off and running. The half-mile tramp along the woods road back to the Cohos Trail gets my blood up. I'm feeling good. A light drizzle keeps the bugs at bay. The cool air makes the walk almost sweat-free. Shortly after those yellow CT trail blazes appear again, the woods road narrows to a well-beaten path that has taken day hikers to the Percy Peaks for decades. It's easy to follow, and the wild forest around me looks quite lovely in the muted morning light. All the understory vegetation – hobblebush, ferns, saplings, moss, etc. – is bright green, rain-soaked and happy. It's a good morning to be in the woods.

"In the presence of nature," Ralph Waldo Emerson once wrote, "A wild delight runs through the man, in spite of real sorrows." Emerson knew what he was talking about, having experienced plenty of loss during his lifetime. That's exactly how I feel right now. Well rested, acclimated to the trail, and grooving on the vibrant green beauty all around me, each breath I take feels like an affirmation of life, a joyous celebration of the natural world. I revel in my own heart-beating existence. Oh sure, I still carry the weight of recent loss, and my creaking joints remind me that I won't be in this world forever, but I am here now and slowly ascending a trail to the Percy Peaks. Life is good. Life in wild places is especially good.

The trail steepens and soon I am scrambling over rocks. My trekking poles are just in the way. It's a dramatic climb, much more rugged than expected. At one point, it takes considerable effort to lift myself over a ledge and up through the rocky crease that's supposed to be a trail. I think of my old dog Matika and what an obstacle this would be for her. I couldn't do it – I couldn't get both her and myself up through this crease at the same time. Good thing she's with me only in spirit. Her spirit weighs nothing.

The trail levels out as it enters a col, then I pass a side trail going to the summit of South Percy Peak. I spot a second side trail coming up from the west. I drop my pack at this junction to study my map. I drink plenty of water and eat as much trail mix as I can while doing so. A thick fog shrouds the surrounding forest. Visibility has been reduced to a few yards. I have hiked into the clouds, and what was drizzle is now just a cool mist against my skin. No wind. No birds. Absolute silence, except for my own heavy breathing. It's quite remarkable, actually. It's almost as if I have climbed into another world.

I pass the side trail to North Percy Peak shortly after resuming my walk. Then it's downhill all the way to Long Mountain Brook. Plenty of slick rocks underfoot, though, so I pay close attention to where I step. All the same, I slip a few times. The rain resumes, making the rocks even slicker. I plant my trekking poles and lean into them while carefully placing my feet. It's an easy descent for the most part, but I slip again, twisting my right ankle hard. I shake it out and continue walking. No big deal. Still I feel a weakness in that ankle that concerns me. Shouldn't be feeling a weakness like this, not with the heavy boots I'm wearing. This is something new, something troubling.

Soon I pass the Percy Loop Tentsite, which consists of one rather large wooden platform. This campsite exists only because the Cohos Trail Association brokered a deal with the State to make hiking through the Nash Stream Forest possible for guys like me. But it's of no use to me this early in the day, so I keep moving.

Upon reaching Long Mountain Brook, I break out my water filter and pump until I have two liters full. The third bottle can go empty now. There's water everywhere so getting more won't be a problem today. A few mosquitoes and black flies annoy me while I pump, but the drizzle resumes so away they go. The drizzle builds to a steady, gentle rain. It's a nice, relatively warm rain. Gotta love it! I could put on my rain jacket but I'd only sweat in it. I don't mind being a little wet. Beats dealing with the bugs – that's for sure. All the same, I break out the waterproof backpack cover and secure it over my pack to keep my things dry.

Beyond the brook, the trail becomes quite interesting. On my new map, it's called the Trio Trail. Freshly cut. Bright yellow rectangular blazes are painted on trees and some saplings have been cut away, but the path underfoot is still covered with forest duff. In fact, there are places where the trail is barely discernable. Only the blazes keep me on track. Much like bushwhacking, except I don't get to pick the easiest possible route through the forest. I tramp across a feeder stream to Long Mountain Brook, then another, then another. There's plenty of water coming down

Long Mountain rising sharply to my right. The trail itself skirts the base of it. The rain is steady now. Relentless might be a better word, actually. No sign of it letting up.

I come upon "Bonnies Pool" after covering some ground. A good water source during a dry summer, no doubt, but I don't need it. So I keep going. The trail turns to the northeast and starts climbing. Soon I am moving in and out of clear-cuts that have been completely stripped of trees but are slowly growing over. Then the trail underfoot becomes an ankle-deep stream soaking my boots. Ah, well... I'm mostly wet anyhow so what difference does it make? Having a little trouble seeing through the raindrops on my eyeglasses, though. Sure would be nice if I had little windshield wipers on them.

The rain continues as I gradually descend to the Trio Ponds Road, slogging through puddles in the low spots of the rain-soaked woods. I cross the muddy road then spot a puncheon-like bridge over the turbulent waters of Pond Brook. The puncheon is covered with chicken wire so my footing is good while I negotiate it. Some trail builder was thinking. Thank you very much! On the other side, the trail descends to Pond Brook Falls. I hear the waterfall roaring long before it pops into view. When it does, I drop my pack then scramble over wet rocks to the base of it, camera in hand. I'm a half-drowned tourist. I snap a couple pictures of the whitewater cataract. The sheer volume of water crashing down before me is both awe-inspiring and intimidating. I am careful where I place my feet, avoiding the slippery edge of the rock that I'm standing on. I'll bet few people have ever seen this much water flowing through here. The falls are a little out of proportion with the chute they have cut through the bedrock.

I reach another road just beyond the falls. This time I'm crossing the narrow, unpaved road that winds through the middle of the Nash Stream Forest. The trailhead on the other side of the road looks strangely familiar. I've been here before – a week and a half ago to be exact. The food bag that I cached before starting this hike is just ahead, on the other side of Nash Stream. It's time to retrieve it.

I stop briefly on the bridge crossing Nash Stream for a good look at the watery wilderness sprawling beneath grey clouds and wrapped in mist. Quite different from the way it looked on that sunny, hot, dusty day ten days ago. Surprisingly enough, Nash Stream isn't running too much higher now than it was then.

On the other side of the bridge, I step out fifty paces to a yellow blaze. Then I count twenty-five more paces beyond it to a large mud hole. I lower my pack to a large flat rock next to the mud hole, using my trekking poles to prop it up. Following a compass bearing due west, I slip through a screen of young conifers, pass between two boulders, and across a rivulet to find a bright yellow bag dangling from a tree limb. Voila! I take it down then return to the trail. I strap the bag to the outside of my pack with a bungee cord I've brought along especially for this occasion. It's raining pretty hard right now so there's no sense opening the bag to inspect its contents. I'll do that later, once I reach Old Hermit Shelter.

A short climb up a wet woods road, then I reach a junction with what looks like another woods road. I stop long enough to check my map and make sure where I'm going. According to my map, the CT is now the Westside ATV Trail. I turn right, following the yellow CT blazes along this pathway. No doubt about it, the Cohos Trail is something else. It is incredibly rugged and barely discernable at times, and a leisurely amble along a woods road at others. A mixed bag. Not boring, that's for sure. Have to keep an eye on those yellow blazes, though. I haven't lost the trail yet, but it would be very easy to do so.

The ATV Trail seems to go on forever. It's late afternoon and I've been on the move for quite some time. I'm tired, slogging through a series of puddles that's supposed to be a trail, and completely soaked to the skin. And the rain is still coming down. "Wow!" is all I can say in response to the relentless rainfall. This is one wet day.

Having reached a gate blocking a side trail, I pull out my map once again to make sure that I'm going the right way. Sure enough I turn here, leaving the ATV Trail. Yellow blazes confirm this. I start climbing the Sugarloaf Arm Trail, which has a stream flowing right through the middle of it. The rain is coming down hard now. Hoo-boy! Water, water everywhere. It's a bit much.

As soon as the trail crests the shoulder of Mt. Sugarloaf, I start looking for a sign pointing to the left. The shelter can't be too far away. I stop briefly to suck down some water, ironically enough. Then I keep going even though I'd like to take a break and get off my feet for a while. There's no good place to do that. Besides, now that I'm completely soaked, it wouldn't take long for me to become chilled. So I keep going. Old Hermit Shelter can't be too far away.

When the trail starts descending, I get serious about looking for a side trail leading to the shelter. It'll pop up any minute now, I keep thinking. But it doesn't. I continue going downhill. Have I missed it? No, I've been looking ever since I crested the shoulder. It'll pop up any minute now. The rain is still coming down hard. I don't even want to think about setting up my tarp on the saturated ground beneath my feet. I have to reach that shelter. It has to be close. Seems like I've gone too far, but no, I've been looking. And there it is! A little brown sign points towards an unseen shelter. "Yee-ha!"

A few moments after leaving the trail, I catch a glimpse of a structure half-hidden by the trees. I race towards it, happier than I've been in a long, long time. Turning the corner of the shelter, I see that it is empty – bone dry and empty. I drop my pack on the shelter floor, leaning it against the wall. Then I hop up right next to it, careful not to spread my wetness around. And just like that, I'm under cover.

10.

"Think before you move," I warn myself. Water is dripping from both my body and my backpack, soaking several square feet of the floor. The rest of the shelter is still dry. I want to keep it that way. So the first thing I do is extract the tarp from deep inside my pack. I unfold it to a large rectangle then lay it out so that I have a place to put all my wet things. I strip down naked next, setting my boots aside and tossing everything else on the tarp. My body is white and wrinkled – the same way it looks whenever I stay in a bathtub too long. I burst out laughing. This is the cleanest I'll be on this trip, no doubt.

I dig a dirty t-shirt from my pack and pat myself dry. The clean, dry clothes that I put on afterward feel heavenly. *This* is why I carry a full change of clothes whenever I'm on the trail for more than a few days at a time. The rain is still coming down hard but I'm dry now, wearing clean dry clothes, inside a dry shelter. And life is good.

I plant my trekking poles in the ground just outside the shelter then throw my soaked backpack cover over it. Deal with that later. Low priority. I string a clothesline across the front of the shelter, just beyond the edge of the shelter floor yet still beneath the roof's overhang. Then I drape all my wet clothes over it. Yeah, I'm taking over this shelter. If someone comes along, I'll have to push all my things aside to make room for them. But I don't expect that to happen. The last entry in the shelter journal is dated June first. Besides, who would be foolish enough to come out here on a day like this?

My backpack is damp on the outside but everything in it is dry. I set up the mosquito bar then place my things along the wall in a nice, tidy row next to it. I'm here for a while, no doubt about that. Tomorrow will be another zero day. Dry out, rest up, and hang out. Why not? I have plenty of time now that I'm only going as far as Dixville Notch. Trekking all the way to Pittsburg is no longer an option. My right ankle is weak, a little swollen and throbbing. That alone is reason enough to take it easy.

Now comes the moment of truth: how have the goods inside my food cache fared during the past ten days? I tear off the duct tape sealing the seams then open the bag. The bag itself is soaked, of course, and there's even water inside the heavy plastic bag lining it. But this food cache has *two* liners and the interior of the second one is bone dry. I chuckle with delight at my cleverness. Then I pull out everything and take an inventory. Remarkably, I have too much food. Haven't been eating enough. Since I'm cutting this trip short and will be exiting the woods at Dixville Notch, I'll have to carry out several unnecessary pounds of food. Hmm… that'll be a first. Not going hungry on this trip, that's for sure.

Speaking of food, it's a cold dinner tonight. I'm tired and don't want to mess around with cooking and cleaning. Besides, I have only one liter of water left and don't want to go out and pump more. There's a small stream very close to the shelter – I can hear it – but I've had enough of being wet for one day. So I fix some lemonade then munch away at beef jerky, sesame sticks, Chex mix and trail mix while reorganizing my food supply. There will be plenty of hot food tomorrow.

After packing up my food bags, I wince at the thought of what comes next. I have to hang them. It's still raining. That means putting on wet boots and pants again. Ugh! A rain jacket and hat keep the upper half of me dry, at least, so going back out isn't too bad. I find a high branch and manage to get a line over it after several failed throws. Then up and away the food bags go for another night. I return to the shelter and immediately switch back into dry clothes again.

There's still plenty of daylight left but I crawl into my sleeping bag anyway. Calling it a day. I write at length in my journal by headlamp before rolling over to sleep. That's when it occurs to me that I haven't seen another person since Karl dropped by at Devil's Rest Shelter yesterday morning. Deep forest solitude. I'm getting a good dose of it. The all-day rain has helped in that regard, no doubt.

Early morning. Once again I awaken to a dripping forest. It rained off and on all night then stopped just before dawn, I think. Hard to say for sure. The forest, completely soaked yesterday, remains soaked. I get out of bed still a bit shaken by an erotic dream. In it my wife Judy was dark skinned. Not quite sure what to make of that. My mother wouldn't have approved that's for sure. Oh well. She's not around any more, sad to say. All the same, I'm confused by the dream. I don't know what it means, if it means anything at all.

A chipmunk chatters from the edge of camp. A blue jay calls in the distance. The vegetation surrounding the shelter is a vibrant green chaos of thriving plants. A cool breeze is blowing steadily from the west. I'm hoping it'll dry things out a bit. My hanging clothes are still wet from yesterday.

First things first. I put on damp pants and boots then go down to the brook to pump water. It's less than fifty yards away. At long last, I've landed in a camp with a convenient water source. The stream is small enough to step over. Might be dry in a dry year but right now it's flowing nicely. I sit cross-legged on a large, flat mossy rock then set to work. The ferns, moss and other vegetation around me are a bright, hallucinogenic green. The tumbling water sings. What a lovely spot! A few gulps of clear, cold water after I've pumped a liter of it and I'm feeling incredibly blessed to be here. I wipe away the water dripping from my beard while looking around. Could the world be any better suited to a creature like me? Could it be any more beautiful?

Back in camp, I fire up the stove and have water boiling for tea faster than it takes to eat a bowl of granola cereal. Then I settle into a dry corner of the shelter, avoiding the damp spot where I landed last night. I'll do a little thinking and journaling this morning while sipping tea and munching an energy bar. I'm looking forward to a long, leisurely day in camp.

Today is Friday, June 21st – the Summer Solstice. It's the longest day of the year. With muted light filtering through the trees from an overcast sky, I'm not feeling it just yet, but I'm sure I will later on when the sun comes out. Something tells me I've seen the last of the rain for a while.

First thought this morning, once I start writing: my trekking days are coming to an end. This trek will be my last one, I believe, though Judy would laugh if she heard me say that. By trekking I mean being on the trail with a heavy pack on my back, tramping fifty to a hundred miles for a week or more. I don't intend to quit going into the woods – not at all – but now that I'm in my 60s, I'm not as enthusiastic about trail pounding as I was twenty years ago, or even ten. Creaky joints, arthritis, and being overweight don't help, but it's more than that. I used to be a big one for climbing mountains. That has lost its appeal over time. Now trekking is also losing its appeal. Neither bagging peaks nor hiking great distances is why I come out here. Not really. Not any more. Now when I go into the woods, I seek something else entirely.

"We live in all we seek," Annie Dillard wrote in one of her more recent books, *For the Time Being*: "The hidden shows up in too plain sight." Yes, that's it. I seek *the hidden*. That's what I'm all about. I am a woods wanderer with an insatiable desire to understand the hidden dimension of the world – what it really is. Every venture of mine into deep woods is a quest. I long to make the spiritual something tangible, to find in the natural world the essence of What-Is. What is real is natural, I believe, and whenever I immerse myself in wild nature I immerse myself in that reality. Hidden in plain sight, absolutely. Reality is no more difficult to encounter than the green chaos all around me right now. Yet making sense of it takes a lifetime.   I'm a wordsmith by trade but find it incredibly difficult to find the right words to describe What-Is even after I have encountered it.   That's because it seems to defy words.   But there's one thing I can say for certain: any concept of What-Is that doesn't take the natural world into account is bullshit.   *This* is the place to begin seeking the hidden – here in this wild, sprawling forest.   And being alone in it is, I believe, the best way to go about that.

Keep it simple.   Elaborate philosophical systems describing What-Is are not necessary.   In fact, they are misleading.   Reality is self-evident.   It is rooted in the basic biological needs of all of us.   That's what makes a trip into a wild forest so instructive.   In the wild one's life is stripped down to its essentials: eating, sleeping, shelter, staying warm and dry, staying healthy, keeping body and soul together.   Life in the woods is simple, and that's the genius of it.   Before we aspire to any lofty notions of what we *ought* to be, we must first acknowledge that we are creatures with basic needs like all other creatures.   Any reasonable understanding of What-Is begins with this simple concept.   Simple yet extremely difficult to grasp.   To be honest, I must say that I'm not quite there yet.   There's a part of me that still wants the word "human" to stand for something more, as if we are gods only pretending to be creatures. Fifty thousand years of self-awareness and pondering What-Is has brought humankind to this salient point.

We presume that we are somehow godlike, and that's precisely what holds us back from completely understanding the world and ourselves.

11.

Late morning. I awaken from a short nap. Drowsiness came on while I was working in my journal. The air has a bit of a chill to it but that won't last. Temps have warmed up considerably since daybreak. A strong wind is blowing my things dry. The wind is making life difficult for the few bugs that are out and about, as well. That's a good thing as far as I'm concerned.

My boots are still wet. The only effective way to dry them out is to wear them. With this in mind, I pull on a pair of dirty but dry socks then slide my feet into the boots and lace them up tightly. The dry socks will speed up the drying process. They also make wearing wet boots tolerable as I putter about camp, tidying up my things. The thought of it is worse than the reality.

Have I actually been in the woods a week already? The first few days were the hardest, when I was still clinging to that urban mindset, to being *civilized*. Comfort and convenience are paramount in the developed lowlands, but over time one can easily adjust to having fewer niceties. Here at Old Hermit Shelter, for example, there's a well-kept, compost outhouse. That seems like a luxury compared to an old-fashioned one. Hell, I don't even need an outhouse. Over the years, I have become quite comfortable digging an eight-inch-deep hole in the forest floor and doing my business there. In fact, I prefer it.

Whenever I'm alone in the forest for any length of time, I go wild. I'm barely aware of this transition, though. It's a subtle change. Slipping into the natural world comes naturally. I don't fight it any more. I just let it happen. I welcome it, actually. I am still myself in every respect, and still consider myself as civilized as anyone else. Yet creature-ness rises to the forefront of my consciousness. I no longer mask it with the pretense of being something else – a divine being of some sort existing more in mind or spirit than body. Consequently, I am more in tune with my surroundings, with the changes in the wind, air temperature, terrain and vegetation. I hear more, see more, and notice more. I revel in the smell of forest duff – that rich, earthy smell of growth and decay that permeates everything. When the thrushes, sparrows and other songbirds sing, I listen. They are more than just white noise. The leaves all around me flutter as tree limbs undulate in the wind, and it's a wonderful thing to behold. The natural world is magnificent in a quiet, unpretentious way. And I feel quite fortunate to be a part of it.

In the wild I think more concretely, making better judgments regarding my physical well being. I also think more freely, allowing my thoughts to run wild. All those rules back in the developed lowlands – the nuts and bolts of any civilized society – seem rather absurd. They are tiresome, actually. They are extraneous out here, entirely unnecessary. Common sense is all I need to get by. And a little human decency is all I need to get along with other people whenever I encounter them. Sometimes rules only get in the way of that.

"Life consists with wildness," Thoreau wrote in his famous essay *Walking*, "The most alive is the wildest." Whenever I am alone in the woods for any length of time, this rings true to me. Back in the developed lowlands, I run around like a rat in a maze and feel somewhat diminished by it. But out here I feel fully alive, wild and free, completely myself. The wild forest suits me better than the city. It is less constricting, that's for sure.

Early afternoon. They're back! While boiling up water and making instant mashed potatoes to augment my usual cold lunch, mosquitoes and black flies try to make lunch out of me. A steady, daylong breeze has dried out the forest so all the bloodsucking insects are airborne again. I pump another liter of water down by the brook to keep up my supply then slip under the net for a while. I prefer being under the net to wearing insect repellent, but I'll have to resort to repellent later on. I'm not going to stay beneath the net the rest of the day.

After carefully studying maps for an hour or so, I firm up plans regarding the rest of my hike. Dixville Notch is twenty miles away. I can do that in two days, with a stay at Baldhead Shelter tomorrow night. I'll exit the woods Sunday afternoon. That'll make it easy for Judy to come pick me up. She won't have to take a day off from work. I could take another zero day at Baldhead Shelter, and/or camp another night somewhere along the high ridge beyond Dixville Peak, but there's no good water source in either place. A weak right ankle effectively rules out going beyond Dixville Notch. I no longer have any desire to do that, anyhow. Nine days on the trail is enough. I don't mind leaving the woods two days early. It's the smart thing to do. Baldhead Shelter is located near the top of Baldhead Mountain so I can probably use my cell phone there to call Judy and arrange a Dixville Notch pickup. If not, I'll call her from the notch. I confirmed cell service there during my scouting trip. Yeah, before even starting this hike, I thought it might come to this.

Late afternoon. I'm growing restless on this my second zero day. That's a good sign. My stomach is growling. That's also a good sign. Getting my strength and appetite back. Most of my gear is dry or nearly dry now, even though there's still a slightly damp spot on the shelter floor where I landed last night. I'll be ready to pack up and make some tracks first thing tomorrow morning. The only remaining issue is my right ankle. I just practiced taping it but didn't like the result. The tape felt too constricting. That's how it's supposed to feel, I suppose, but I don't like it. So I immediately tore off the tape, resolving to go without it as long as possible.

The surrounding forest emanates all kinds of sounds. I do my best to identify them. That's a nuthatch nearby. That's a wood frog, I think. That's a tree limb falling in the distance. What's that squeal? What's that thumping sound? "Do not analyze the voices of the woods too acutely, or they disintegrate," the mid-20th century naturalist Sam Campbell said, "Let them have their mystery." But I want to know every creak, rattle and groan. No, what I really want is to be surprised by a critter suddenly appearing – one I haven't seen in years: a bear, a wildcat, a moose or something. Yet most of the wildlife around me remains hidden behind a screen of green. Hmm…

To live with mystery is an inescapable aspect of being human. We are sapient creatures but we don't know everything. Some people are happy enough living with this unknowing, but I want things explained. That's the philosopher in me, I suppose. I ask questions – lots and lots of questions. I can't leave any rock unturned. Yet overturning rocks is the best way to perpetuate mystery. The more we learn about particulars, the less we know about the whole. The forest hides behind the trees.

The greatest mystery, of course, is my human-ness. I am both an animal and something else. It's a mind-boggling paradox. I have been told many times that I think too much, and it's true I do. But the same could be said about my entire species. Collectively speaking, *Homo sapiens* think too much. We keep overturning rocks, learning more and more about the natural world while remaining befuddled about both our own nature and the nature of the universe at large. I am an animal and something else. I am both natural and unnatural. I am both wild and civilized. What does all this mean? What am I really?

When alone in deep woods, I feel connected. I am a part of the natural world. To a pantheist like myself, who believes that God and nature are one in the same, it seems like I am a part of God. Clearly I'm not the only one who feels this way. "The currents of the Universal Being circulate through me," Emerson wrote in his beautiful little book called *Nature*, "I am a part or particle of God." It is a feeling that many people have, no doubt, when immersed in the wild. In the natural world, everything is connected to everything else. Alone in the wild, it is easy to become aware of this, to realize that we too are a part of nature. And when a mosquito or a black fly escapes my hand, making off with a drop of my blood, the reality of this is driven home.

My mother is dead now yet she remains a part of nature, as do all the creatures that have ever lived. Her body has returned to the universe at large. Her spirit persists, as do the spirits of all things, as part of the Great Spirit itself – that from which all things flow. I do not have to wait until I die to rejoin my mother or the other spirits of once-living things. They are all with me here and now. They are a part of me and I am a part of them. The universe is one, by definition, and it is all mixed together. Galaxies, stars, planets, living things, atoms, particles – it is all one. I forget this fact whenever I focus on the particulars. I forget about Oneness whenever I am blinded by my own sense of individuality – this breathing, walking, thinking ecosystem of interdependent cells and microorganisms that I call myself. But when I am paying attention, *really* paying attention, it becomes obvious to me that nothing stands alone.

Evening. After cooking up and eating some ramen noodles along with some trail mix and an energy bar, I repack all my food into one bag. I put my trash in the other one. Then I sling the bags back into the trees. A quick trip down to the brook and I have three bottles full of water again. With the exception of a nasty pair of wool socks, my clothes are dry. And the blisters on my feet are patched. Everything is squared away. I am ready to hit the sack then rise to another big hiking day. But the sun is still high in the sky. This is indeed the longest day of the year. It'll be another hour or two before the sun goes down.

I listen to songbirds, the wind whispering through the trees, and the steady rush of the nearby stream. All physical hardships aside, it feels great to be out here, grooving on the wild. It feels spiritually cleansing. It's hard to keep from daydreaming in deep forest solitude, and that's probably the best reason for being here. Daydreams are good for the soul. What was it that had me so stressed out the night before I entered the forest? I don't recall. It doesn't matter.

If someone had asked me a week ago what the point is of being out here, I would have been hard-pressed to give a good answer. Now it's obvious to me. The point is to learn gratitude. I am thankful for being alive in such a harsh yet beautiful world. I first learned this while I was sojourned alone in the Alaskan bush a couple decades ago. But every once in a while, it seems, I need to relearn it. Life in the developed lowlands bleaches out this wild memory.

The beauty of the world lies in the interconnectedness of all things – in what we call natural order. There is chaos in the world, surely, but all is not chaos. The universe is the dance of order and chaos. While sitting in a shelter deep in the woods, scribbling in my journal, it becomes painfully obvious to me what I *don't* know about this dance. I am only a woods wanderer with a sketchy understanding of nature and my place in it. I speculate about what I don't know, thus making a fool of myself. I ask questions for which there are no definitive answers. My worldview is chock full of unanswerable questions. A random universe or an ordered one – what does anyone know about it all, about causation? And it always comes down to that. "Beauty" is simply the word that comes to mind whenever I experience the natural world firsthand. It's my way of saying that nature is a good thing, despite all its disasters, diseases and other unpleasant aspects. But what do I really know about the machinations of the universe? In that regard, I'm just another not-quite-so-sapient creature.

12.

Saturday, July 22nd. Day eight. I'm up with the sun and feeling good. Excited about getting back on the trail. Slept well last night despite a few unexpected breaks in the forest silence. Went down with the sun yesterday after scribbling in my journal, falling asleep to thrush songs. The roar of ATVs filled the air shortly after dark. It seemed like those four-wheeled vehicles were only a few yards away from the shelter, but they were probably running up and down Nash Stream Road. That's half a mile away as the bird flies. In the middle of the night, a wooden door awakened me repeatedly as it opened then slammed shut. Really now. The bears should be a little more considerate when they use the outhouse.

A bowl of cereal and hot tea for breakfast, a little stretching, a long look at my maps, then I'm ready to move. I pack up my things and hit the trail with two liters of water left over from yesterday. The sun shines brightly through the broadleaf trees. That and patches of blue sky promise a fair day. My backpack probably weighs close to forty-five pounds again, after retrieving that food cache the day before yesterday. Haven't eaten much during this hike so now I'm carrying extra food. Oh well. Better than not having enough, I suppose.

The Sugarloaf Arm Trail, following what was once a woods road, is an easy downhill walk. It's still wet and muddy from Thursday's soaker, though, along with all the rain that has fallen since early spring. An incredibly wet year. My boots were almost dry earlier this morning, but now they are wet again. So it goes. I carefully plant my trekking poles when crossing a few particularly muddy spots, making sure not to slip and fall. Yeah, I've kissed the ground enough for one outing.

It feels good to be moving again, to be breathing deeply and just barely breaking a sweat while cruising downhill. Hiking through the forest is delightful when the trail is effortless, the weather is fair, and the bugs aren't menacing. I revel in it. This morning I'm a happy hiker without a care in the world.

Soon the trail underfoot flattens out. That's when I hear people shouting not far away. I spot them a couple minutes later, thus ending a three-day spell of deep woods solitude. There are a bunch of them moving this way and that along both sides of the trail. I'm not quite sure what they're doing. They look young – late teens, maybe early twenties. I spot their camp right next to the Nash Stream. I guess no one told them that they're not supposed to camp here. I stop and hail the closest ones with a friendly "Hello!" A young woman returns my greeting as she comes over to chat. The rest are aloof. The young woman, somewhat older than the rest, is the group leader. This is an Outward Bound group, she tells me. There are ten of them, including herself and another group leader. They started at Dixville Notch the day before yesterday, and stayed the first night at Baldhead Lean-to. Glad I didn't land there when they did. That said it's nice to encounter people again. It's also nice to say goodbye after a short, pleasant chat then walk away.

I cross a wooden bridge over Nash Stream, then cross the Nash Stream Road. I spot yellow blazes on the other side of the road and follow them along what is called the East Side Trail. That's east as in east of the Nash Bog. The bog is a haven for moose, I'm sure. Soon I am dodging large piles of moose pellets dumped on the trail. I cut my pace, moving as quietly as possible, hoping to spot moose in the brush ahead. The trail meanders in and out of clearings where it's easy to imagine them hanging out. But no large furry animal pops into view. After covering some ground, I reach a side trail leading to the bog. I detour down it, hoping to spot a moose foraging there. No such luck. I resume my northward trek a little disappointed, even though I know that wildlife rarely appears on queue.

Just before dropping onto the Nash Stream Road as indicated on my map, the trail suddenly veers away to the northeast. I'm confused. What's going on here? I call it a trail but it's hardly that. The bright yellow blazes are unmistakable but there's no real path underfoot. The fresh stumps of saplings and bushes are sure signs that this trail has recently been blazed. And I mean *very* recently. I follow the sketchy trail uphill and across hummocky terrain, a bit perturbed at being led away from the road. I grunt and groan and mutter curses under my breath at the trailblazers who cut this path, certain that they didn't know what they were doing. But soon I hear Pike Brook rushing nearby. Then I drop onto the dirt road. There's a gate in sight. Now I get it. I just hiked a brand new section of trail bypassing the last half a mile of the Nash Stream Road. All the same, I don't understand why it winds all over the place.

After spotting a yellow blaze on the other side of the gate, I drop my pack and take a long break to drink, snack and study my maps. The woods road directly ahead leads to Gadwah Notch. It's a nine-hundred-foot climb between here and the notch, stretched over several miles. That shouldn't be too difficult. But when the woods road ends, I'm sure things will get interesting. I gulp down half a liter of water then pack up and go.

As expected, the woods road beyond the gate is easy to follow and the grade isn't bad at all. I stop occasionally to catch my breath, puttering along at a slow, steady pace as if I have all day to reach Baldhead Lean-to. And I do. What the heck, why rush? There are eleven miles of trail between Old Hermit Shelter and Baldhead Lean-to, but I got an early start this morning and am well rested after a second zero day. Slow and steady will get it done.

A mile past the gate, I reach a meadow. Cathedral Meadow it's called on my map. Quite alluring. The trail skirts it. A mile later I come to another clearing called Moran Meadow that's even more alluring – all grassy with an expansive view of the surrounding mountains. But I don't stop. The trail veers off to the right, away from the meadow. I am focused on the steady climb and want to keep moving. All the same, I marvel at the variety of landscapes the Cohos Trail passes through. Stay on this trail long enough, I'm convinced, and one will see just about everything the Great North Woods has to offer.

Another short climb and suddenly the woods road levels out, becoming a long, narrow, grassy corridor. This meadow isn't indicated on my new map, but on my old one it's called Muise Bowl. I drop my pack in the middle of it, just to sit for a while and enjoy the view. Puffy white clouds drift across the azure sky. Conifers cover the high ridge off to my left that sweeps around to a dip ahead that must be Gadwah Notch. Patches of bluets, violets and wild strawberry are scattered across the grass. I break out my food bag and eat lunch while basking in the sunlight. A few black flies come around to annoy me, but they're not so bad. There is nothing but wild forest around me as far as I can see. Oh yeah, this is why I come out here. I have a beautiful high valley all to myself on a glorious summer day. Life doesn't get any better than this. I thank the gods of the mountains for bestowing such good fortune upon me. Then I pack up and continue my hike.

The clearing ends a quarter mile beyond where I took my lunch break. Conifers close in from both sides. I keep my eyes fixed on yellow blazes as the trail becomes muddled in moose paths going every which way. I reach a small brook – the headwaters of Nash Stream – and not a moment too soon. I've nearly finished my last liter. I drop my pack then pick a path through a thick tangle of spruce to reach a small pool where I can easily pump water. Mosquitoes are waiting for me there, of course, so I take a few hits while filling my bottles. When I'm done, I shoulder the heavy pack again, bracing myself for the final ascent into Gadwah Notch.

I pass yet another clearing on my way uphill. It's just a bit too rocky to be called a meadow. According to my old map this is Bulldozer Flats. Veering away from it, the trail narrows as it climbs into

Gadwah Notch, roughly 3,000 feet above sea level. Goodbye Nash Stream watershed. The notch is boreal, thick with conifers, dark and very wet. Fortunately, some puncheon has been laid over the wettest spots so getting through the notch isn't difficult. Easier than I thought it would be, anyhow. I get a little mud on my boots, that's all.

On the other side of the notch, the trail descends to a high ridge leading to Baldhead Mountain. Waist-high ferns obscure the trail in places, making it more important than ever to keep an eye on those yellow blazes. There are plenty of them and they are very fresh. A trail maintenance crew must have come through here recently.

When the trail leaves the ridge, dropping fast downhill, I grumble. Every foot I descend now will only have to be regained as I climb up Baldhead. I lose fifty feet, a hundred then two hundred. Finally the hemorrhage of elevation ends. I stop and check my map one last time. Hmm… Now it's a six-hundred-foot climb up to the Baldhead Lean-to. With ten miles behind me, I'm tired. But today's hike isn't over yet. One more mile left to go.

Mid-afternoon. I creep ever so slowly up Baldhead Mountain. Actually I'm headed for a summit called Baldhead South, which is a quarter mile south of Baldhead Mountain and a few hundred feet higher, oddly enough. Along the way I pass a roll of chicken wire with a can of paint next to it. There must be a trail maintenance crew out here somewhere. I wonder if/when I'll run into them.

To my pleasant surprise, I stumble upon a tiny stream cutting through the rocks. The trail goes right over it. According to my map, the last dependable source of water was the headwaters of Nash Stream that I tapped on the other side of Gadwah Notch. But this has been a wet year and water is flowing nicely here. So I pull out my water filter and top off a bottle. Might as well take advantage of the situation, thus reaching the Baldhead Lean-to fully loaded.

The last half a mile is an agonizing slog – up and up, then up and down and up again over the boulder-strewn ground atop Baldhead South. I am exhausted. So when I catch the flash of light off a shelter's metal roof, I let out a great big sigh of relief. Then I hear people talking. It's only 4 o'clock in the afternoon but a group has already settled in here. When I pop into the clearing in front of the lean-to, I spot them: a man and woman about my age, and two teenage girls. Looks like it's going to be a social evening.

13.

I drop my backpack in front of Baldhead Lean-to and immediately engage in conversation with my companions for the evening. The man is fastening boards to the front of the shelter, with some assistance from the woman. I introduce myself then ask their names. His name is Tom. Hers is Pat. The two teenage girls are their granddaughters, Annalee and Misty. Tom is a little chubbier than me and sports a white beard that's bushier than my grey one. He also wears eyeglasses as I do, as so many older people do. But he's no rocking chair grandpa. He seems to have the energy of a fellow half his age. He works at a good clip, anyhow, weatherizing the shelter. Pat is quiet, something of an introvert. She lets Tom do all the talking. The girls are typical teenagers, friendly enough yet just a tad aloof.

I tell Pat and Tom that I hail from Vermont and am currently hiking the Cohos Trail from Jefferson to Dixville Notch. Tom says that he and his two granddaughters hiked a good portion of it as well, from the Canadian border south to Emerson. Pat met them along the way and kept them supplied. Tom couldn't get enough time away from work to hike the entire trail but he hopes to finish it someday. As far as backpacking goes, they are newcomers. Tom took Annalee bird hunting three years ago, and when they came to a beautiful hilltop she told him that she wanted to camp there. They started backpacking right after that, doing their hike on the CT with Misty the following year. Incredible. Clearly Tom isn't one of those people going gently into old age. Makes wonder why I should.

Right now Tom and his crew are out for the weekend doing trail maintenance. They hauled wood and other materials up an unmarked side trail that joins the CT a mile back, right before it ascends to Baldhead. That was their chicken wire and can of paint I saw earlier. Tom is a very active member of The Cohos Trail Association (TCTA). In addition to being on its board, he comes out here and does trail work. I'm impressed. His enthusiasm for the CT greatly surpasses my own. He's giving back in a major way. And he has made it a family affair.

Tom and Pat live and work in Maine. She does kitchen work at a school. He works as a draftsman in a machine shop. But Tom's heart is still in northern New Hampshire. He grew up in Berlin, not more than thirty miles from here as the bird flies, and spends as much time on the Cohos Trail as he can. His granddaughters are with him more often than not. I'm envious. I've spent some time in the woods with my grandkids, but not nearly as much as I'd like. Half of my grandkids live in southern New Hampshire, and the other half live in Virginia. That makes planning outings with them a bit tricky.

I ask Tom, Pat and the girls if I can settle into the far right corner of the shelter. I like being against the wall. They push all their gear to the left, making room for me. I set up my mosquito bar first thing. They find it somewhat amusing. The net is a godsend in a buggy season like this, I tell them, and they can relate to that. But it's obvious from their response that they've never seen anything like it before.

Baldhead Lean-to faces into the prevailing winds, Tom tells me. At 3,000 feet, those winds can be pretty nasty sometimes. That is why boards have been slapped across the front of the shelter in a rather makeshift way. He's basically finishing the job, adding a few more boards, transforming the lean-to into a cabin of sorts with a four-foot-wide opening. Completed in back in 2003, this shelter is beginning to show its age. But that hardly matters. It's a godsend for hikers like me.

After settling into my corner of the shelter, I go out and sling my food bag in the trees a short distance down the trail. Tom does the same after setting up a hammock in an open space about twenty yards away from the shelter. That's where Misty is going to sleep. Wild girl. She's going barefoot right now, but Pat and Tom keep telling her that she'll need to wear socks and more clothes when she goes to bed this evening. Temps have already dropped into the 60s and it'll get a lot colder up here tonight, especially in the hammock. Misty says she'll be fine.

Tom breaks out a camp stove and starts dinner. I do the same. As we eat, our conversation revolves around the many challenges of creating a new trail system like the CT in this day and age. Bureaucracy, the concerns of landowners, and the conflicting interests of various groups confound even the simplest plans. That brand new section of trail to Pike Brook, for example – the one going uphill for no apparent reason – was the result of parameters established by the State. The trail has to stay a good distance away from the road and so on. My head explodes as Tom tries to explain it all to me. So we change the topic while cleaning up, talking about the many delights of being in the woods. That I can handle.

Soon everyone is settling in for the night. I'm tired and have another big hiking day ahead of me. Tom, Pat and the girls discuss the trail work they'll be doing tomorrow before heading out. A cool breeze blows right before dusk, making me appreciate the boards that Tom has nailed to the front of the shelter. I write in my journal before going to sleep, recounting the day's adventures.

Cell phone service on Baldhead is a little sketchy, but I managed to get a text out to Judy shortly after reaching the lean-to. I let her know that I'll be exiting the woods at Dixville Notch tomorrow afternoon. Could she come pick me up? She responded a short while later, saying that she could. Judy was surprised to hear that I'm cutting the trip short. I told her I'm fine, that she shouldn't worry. Details later. I'll text her again from Table Rock, around midday tomorrow. Nine days is enough, I said, ending the thread on that note. Is that true? I wonder while nodding off. Nine days will have to be enough. All day today, I've been ignoring the obvious. The throb in my right ankle is only getting worse. I have to leave the trail.

Daybreak. I slept fitfully last night. My entire body is sore. Thanks to a colon ulcer that I got a several years ago from taking too much ibuprofen, I don't use painkillers any more. No doubt that explains my heightened sensitivity to aches and pains during this outing – especially joint pain. I used to rely heavily on ibuprofen during long treks. I just tough it out nowadays. As my old hiking buddy John likes to say, the pain is proof that I'm still alive. Yeah, that sort of twisted stoicism keeps me going.

It's chilly this morning, as expected. I'm nice and warm in my sleeping bag and see no reason to get up right away. Besides, everyone else is sleeping and I don't want to disturb them. My mind races in the early morning twilight. So I grab my headlamp and journal, then scribble away…

It feels good to be in the woods again. I'm thankful for being able to come out here, and am glad to be doing this hike despite all the aches, pains and other mortifications of the flesh. But I'm just a tad surprised by my poor performance on the trail. That's partly due to not being in the best shape, and partly due to the aging process. I could pretend that I'm immortal and go about my business accordingly, but that doesn't fly out here. No, I'm an old hiker now. That's okay. I'm a young old, though. Only in my early 60s, I can probably hike for another decade or so, maybe longer. In the future I'll dial back the mileage and do shorter trips. No sense pushing it. Any way to be in the woods is a good way. Just being out here is life affirming. The key is to keep moving no matter what, and to live life to its fullest, enjoying all the wonder and beauty that the natural world has to offer. That said I'm almost ready to exit the woods. Almost. Another nine miles of trail pounding today and I'll be completely ready, I'm sure.

Tom stirs from his bed and soon everyone is up and at it. Misty shows up with her sleeping bag, chilled after a long night in the hammock. She wraps it around her shoulders then curls into a corner of the shelter. I painstakingly wrap my right ankle with sports tape then get dressed. The tape feels constricting, but there's no doubt in my mind now that I need it. The ankle is swollen and sensitive to the touch.

A granola bar, hot tea and a bowl of cereal. Then as much trail mix as I can eat. Fueling up for the hike ahead. I finish off the water in a second bottle, leaving me with one more. That'll get me to the stream in Kelsey Notch were I can refill. I break camp, systematically stuffing gear into my backpack then hoisting the load to my sore shoulders. Tom, Pat and the girls are still puttering about camp. They are in no rush to leave. But I'm ready now for one last big hike. I wish them all the best then grab my trekking poles and go.

14.

The trail from Baldhead to Kelsey Notch is downhill all the way. Smooth sailing for the most part, except for a few boggy places where it's easy to slip and fall. I plant my trekking poles firmly to avoid that while I hike. I fall down once anyway, slipping on a patch of sloped mud where it looks like others have slipped before. I'm not hurt but now the lower half of my pants are nearly as muddy as my boots. It's more frustrating than worrisome. When I was thirty, I was so nimble, so light on my feet that I practically danced down the trail. But now it's a slog, with me hitting the ground on a regular basis. Sturdy trekking poles, good tread on my boots, and paying close attention. Yet still I fall.

Halfway down the trail, I come into a small glade full of waist-high ferns awash in sunlight, surrounded by short, dark spruces and a few spindly, towering birches. Through the birches I see the hazy top of Dixville Peak a few miles to the northeast. It looks far away, but I'll be ascending that mountain a couple hours from now. Here in northern New England, mountains are never as far away as they appear. Dixville Peak is the last climb on this trek of mine. I have mixed feelings about that. The exhausted old duffer in me wants only to be on the other side of it and done with this hike. But my wilder self doesn't like the idea of leaving the trail, going back to the developed lowlands. My wilder self wants to keep going all the way to Canada.

In the middle of the morning, I set foot on a wide, well-maintained dirt road cutting through Kelsey Notch. I follow the road eastward, looking for a place to draw water. I spot a pool in a tiny stream flowing through a large culvert beneath the road. This'll do, even though the West Branch of Clear Stream is somewhere not far ahead. I leave my pack on the road then drop down to the pool to pump water. It's a short yet very steep descent. The loose ground gives away with each step I take. No matter. A short while later, I'm back on the road with enough water to finish my hike. I drink a little of it and munch an energy bar while studying my maps. But I don't linger. The sun shines brightly through a mostly clear sky, quickly warming the air, so the black flies are coming out. Best to keep moving.

Sure enough, I pass the West Branch of Clear Stream shortly after refilling my bottles. Then it's a steady climb up the road to a junction with another dirt road. Lots of signs at this junction telling travelers what lies in which direction, including a CT marker pointing up the narrower, rock-strewn dirt road. I follow it towards Dixville Peak. According to my map, I'll gain six hundred feet elevation on this road before leaving it a quarter mile short of the peak. I brace myself for the climb.

I commence a turtle-like creep uphill, stopping frequently to catch my breath. Just then four ATVs come roaring up the road in single file. Three of the ATVs have male drivers with women accompanying them. One fellow rides alone. I wave as they pass. They all wave back. About twenty minutes later, they pass me again on their way downhill. I'm still puttering along. No doubt my slow ascent looks grueling to those sitting comfortably on fast-moving vehicles. But a hike like mine is life affirming. As tough as it is, I wouldn't have it any other way. I don't know what they get out of their ride. They all seem to be enjoying themselves. To each his or her own.

I spot another CT trail marker right where the dirt road steepens and turns sharply to the right. It points into the woods. I drop my pack and take a long, well-deserved break before leaving the road. The tips of several wind turbines atop Dixville Peak sweep over the treetops. It would be cool to walk beneath them, but that's probably what the newly cut Dixville Bypass Trail just ahead is all about. Some trailblazer determined that it was better to avoid those turbines *before* permission to pass beneath them was taken away. That's my best guess, anyhow. The Cohos Trail passes through mostly private land between here and the Canadian border. Keeping it open for hikers like me in the years to come will be challenging, I'm sure.

The Dixville Bypass is a steep descent at first. Then it becomes a nightmare rollercoaster trail, twisting and turning through the dense forest, clinging to the side of the mountain with virtually no trail work done to it at all. I try not to be too judgmental, well aware that my current state of exhaustion is warping my perception of things. Still I can't help but think that a better route could have been blazed through here – one following the contours on my map. All the way, I hear the *whoosh! whoosh!* of unseen wind turbine blades slicing through the air, along with the low hum of energy being captured. What a strange combination: advanced technology and wild forest.

Shortly after the trail flattens out, it empties into a rough, heavily eroded woods road headed for Dixville Peak. I find a yellow blaze painted on a rock leading the other way, downhill. I'm a bit concerned by the sudden appearance of this road. There's no road indicated on my map, and it loses elevation fast. As I am walking down it, I search for another yellow marker but don't see one. I backtrack to where the trail exits the woods, carefully scanning the other side of the road for an opening in the trees. Nothing. So I continue going downhill until finally I find another yellow marker on bedrock. This one assures me that I'm going the right way. With Judy en route to pick me up, this wouldn't be a good time to get turned around. When finally I find a blaze pointing back into the woods, I let out a great big sigh of relief.

While I'm glad to be back in the woods again, with the Cohos Trail unquestionably underfoot, the sketchy overgrown woods road that I'm now following is extremely wet. There are low boggy places bracketed by thick stands of spruce that are impossible to avoid. I sink calf-deep in muck a couple times, reminded once again what a rainy year this has been. And the black flies are having their way with me, of course. I stopped to slather on bug dope back on the Dixville Bypass Trail, but that isn't making much difference now. I've sweated away most of it. No matter. I keep moving, waving the flies away as I tramp along.

Suddenly the forest gives way to an open ridgeline with a couple old buildings, a ski-lift terminus, and several wide grassy lanes sloping downward. I have just entered the Balsams Wilderness Ski Area. It feels strange being here, like I'm trespassing or something. There isn't a living soul in sight, which makes being here feel even stranger. I drop my pack at the base of some stairs leading to a hut, then pull out my map. Once again the yellow blazes are few and far between. I want to make sure that I don't miss the CT's reentry into the woods. A little study and a few gulps of water later, I have a pretty good idea which way to go. I shoulder my pack and follow a broad, descending ski trail for a while, pleased when I spot a yellow blaze off to the side of it. Then I leave the ski trail for a much narrower path slipping back into the forest shadows.

Table Rock, that dramatic overlook above Dixville Notch that I've read about, can't be more than a mile away. I'm exited about reaching it so I pick up my pace. That's a mistake. The trail underfoot is almost as wet and boggy as the one on the other side of the ski area, and soon I'm paying the price for my enthusiasm. Down I go, twisting my left ankle in the process. With my right ankle wrapped, I favor my other leg whenever the footing looks precarious. So now my left ankle is tweaked, as well. No doubt about it, I'm reaching the end of my tether. Hiking beyond Dixville Notch wouldn't be possible now even if I wanted to do it. Leaning into my trekking poles, I pick myself up and keep going. Sixty miles behind me, only a few left to go.

One last bit of uphill effort then I cruise down the trail to a sign pointing towards Table Rock. I drop my pack at the sign before heading down the short, rocky side trail with a camera in hand. Whoa! Before me is a long, narrow, rocky precipice reaching way out over Dixville Notch with a five-hundred-foot drop on both sides. I creep out as far as I dare to go on wobbly legs and weak ankles. Vertigo is setting in so I squat down to snap a few pictures. The regal looking Balsams Resort is in the valley to the left. The notch itself is off to the right. The cars on the road passing through the notch look like tiny bugs. A sheer rock face on my right, half hidden in the shadows, plummets towards the road. Sanguinary Mountain rises sharply on the other side of the notch, into a partly cloudy sky. It's a magnificent view, but I don't feel like lingering. I return to my pack dropped on the CT where I can sit down and relax.

I pull out a food bag, maps and a last liter of water while resting my back against a tree. I pour a little lemonade powder into a cup then add water to it. Yes sir, I'm having a picnic. And why not? It's a short, downhill hike to the notch from here. No rush. Almost finished. I pull out my cell phone and text a message to Judy, letting her know where I am. A few minutes later she texts back, telling me that she's on her way. It's one o'clock. My estimated time of arrival at the trailhead is 2:30, I text back. Then I put the phone away. One last entry in my journal then I groove on the wild all around me while slowly finishing lunch.

15.

Not out of the woods yet. Still another mile and a half to go. I heft the leaden pack to my shoulders and slip my arms into its straps, snapping the belt into place then tightening it to shift some of the load to my hips. My shoulders, hips, knees and ankles are all sore, and I'm stiff from sitting for half an hour. I stab the ground with my trekking poles while firing up the mental fortitude for one last push. It won't be that hard, I tell myself. Dixville Notch is downhill from here, all the way. I grunt over a short yet unexpected rise in the trail then begin the thousand-foot descent.

It's a beautiful summer afternoon, with an ovenbird breaking the forest silence and the surrounding vegetation undulating in a faint breeze. I catch myself daydreaming about the coming reunion with Judy, my partner for the past thirty-odd years. Am really missing her now. After our brief exchange of texts at Table Rock, I long to hear her voice. But the trail is dropping fast so I had better pay attention to it. I focus on the here/now, carefully placing my feet and trekking poles as I descend, watching for those subversive little roots and rocks that want to catch the toe. Though harder on the joints than going uphill, going downhill like this is easy on the lungs. So I start humming. Then I whistle a few tunes as if life stripped down to its basics is a good thing. And it is.

I hear the rush of running water long before seeing it. The sound grows louder as I approach a deep cut in the terrain. After crossing the stream, I follow the trail as it turns sharply to the left. Then it hugs the ravine. There are plenty of blazes to keep me on track, but the going is a little tougher now with the trail twisting and turning every which way. When the rush of water builds to a roar, I know the Huntington Cascades are close. I catch a glimpse of whitewater in the deep cut off to my left. I drop the pack and fish out my camera. Then I walk over to the edge and gaze into a gorge where one waterfall drops to another in rapid succession. I snap a few pictures of the cascades but something will be lost in translation, I'm sure. The hypnotic beat of water crashing against rock, the smell of ozone, and the sheer magnitude of the cascades – none of this can be captured by an image. So I simply enjoy it for a while before moving on.

Shortly after shouldering my pack and resuming the hike, I spot a couple about my age on the trail below. They are creeping uphill ever so slowly, smiling and unencumbered. They are obviously here for the falls. They shout hello. I return the greeting. No doubt noticing the big pack on my back, as well as signs of exhaustion in my face, they quickly conclude that I've been out for a while. They say something to that effect. I only half hear it, responding with "Oh yeah, it's been a trip." Then I point out the obvious, that the waterfalls are just ahead.

When the trail levels out, it starts looking strangely familiar. I walked this far into the woods back in 2014 while I was scouting the Dixville Notch trailhead. Had my dog Matika with me then, of course. Her ghost follows me out of the woods. The trail empties into a parking lot. There's only one car parked here. I follow the access road past an old family cemetery, CT blazes marking the path northward, and a green salt shed, until I reach a paved road. Then I drop my pack on its shoulder. I have arrived. 62 miles and nine days later, my trek on the Cohos Trail is over.

Now waiting for pickup. I sit down, making myself comfortable in the grass just beyond the road's gravel shoulder. Cars race past at ridiculous speeds – blasts of air in their wake drying the sweat on my brow. I keep an eye peeled for my wife's red car coming out of Dixville Notch. Nothing yet. Just a couple false alarms. Red cars are common. So I start thinking about my recently deceased mother, wondering what she would say if she were still alive and could see me now. Congratulations? No, she would ask me if I had a good time. After giving the matter some thought, I would have to say yes. No doubt about it, backpackers like me are a strange lot. The tougher the hike, the more we enjoy it.

I catch another flash of red coming out of the notch. It starts looking familiar as it approaches. Sure enough that's Judy's car. It slows down, turns onto the access road then stops. I grab my pack and chase it. I give Judy a great big hug and kiss as soon as she steps out of the car. Then the transformation begins, from solitary woods walker to a more civilized version of myself.

Judy has a set of my street clothes and a plan for us to stop by a restaurant on the way home. Sounds good. But my hair is disheveled and wild looking. She's not going anywhere with me looking like this. I strip off my sweaty t-shirt and lean forward so that she can douse my head with the remaining half a liter of my drinking water. Then she combs it until I stop her. I dry my hair with the sweaty t-shirt then wipe my body down with it after stripping off the rest of my dirty clothes. The clean street clothes smell fresh. They feel good against my skin. Judy asks what happened as I peel away the tape from my right ankle. I tell her I've had more trouble with my ankles than my knees on this trip. She's surprised to hear it.

Judy hands me a bottle of ice water that I suck down after stowing my pack in the trunk of the car. Then she opens a cooler to display its contents: a beer, a soda, and iced green tea. Does she love me, or what? I grab the bottle of tea then slip into the passenger's seat of the car. Judy's driving us home and that's a good thing. I'm in no frame of mind to drive.

The car rolls down the highway. Judy listens patiently while I ramble on and on. She knows the routine, how I always unload after a big trip. I talk all the way out of New Hampshire and halfway across Vermont. It's a litany of hardships, grief, and the mortification of flesh that sounds pretty bad, so I assure her that it was a great hike through wild, beautiful country providing all the deep woods solitude that I so desperately needed. Then I announce that I won't be trekking this long and hard again. Judy scoffs, having heard that before. "No, this time I'm serious," I say, but she doesn't believe it for a second.

Soon we are in Newport, approaching the East Side Restaurant. Judy parks the car. We go inside and are seated on the deck overlooking Lake Memphremagog. A gentle breeze blows across the lake as the sun plays peekaboo behind a few passing clouds. The place is nearly full. A musician sings while strumming his guitar at the opposite end of the deck. I order a hamburger, fries and a root beer. When the meal comes, I marvel at it. It looks delicious but seems like a terrible indulgence after nine days of trail fare. I wolf it down all the same.

Back in the car, Judy starts talking about her public health job and how much she's looking forward to retirement in two months. She talks most of the way home. Once that subject is exhausted, I ask how my 90-year-old father is doing. There's no news from Ohio, she says, though my sister is still worried about him living alone. His dementia is only getting worse. No surprise there. I'll call him tomorrow.

As soon as we get back home, I blow open my pack in the garage. I hang my sleeping bag, tarp, and ground cloth on a clothesline then scatter the rest of my gear across the floor. I'll get back to all this tomorrow. I'll wash my clothes and salvage what I can of the trail food at that time, as well. I take a shower and it's absolutely heavenly – ribbons of steaming water washing away nine days of grime. Drinking water is as easy as turning a faucet handle. The bed feels almost too soft when I lie down on it. Yes sir, the creature comforts are coming fast now that I'm out of the woods.

It takes a few days to get back into the swing of things. I pick up my book biz where I left it, check my email, and sort through the photos taken during the trip. Eventually, I clean up my gear and put it away. I still feel the loss of my mother and my dog, but it's not so bad now that I'm back in the regular routine. That said, it'll take some doing to fully process the thoughts and feelings I had about them and other deceased loved ones while I was on the trail. My world has been shaken by these deaths. I call my father only to find out that he is still teetering on the precipice. Urinary blockage, dizziness and internal bleeding in addition to heart trouble and dementia. Hard to say how much longer he'll be with us. My attitude towards death has been altered to some extent by the hike I just did. My own mortality factors into the mix somehow. Hard to say what I'll ultimately make of it all. Right now, I know only one thing for certain: nature persists. The planet continues spinning despite the coming and going of the countless life forms on it. I am both horrified and consoled by this simple fact. Despite diseases, disasters and everything else, life goes on.

About the Author

Walt McLaughlin received a degree in philosophy from Ohio University in 1977 and has been wondering, wandering and writing ever since. He has over a dozen books in print, including a narrative about his immersion in the Alaskan bush, *Arguing with the Wind*, and one about backpacking through the Adirondacks, *The Allure of Deep Woods*. He is also the force behind a small press called Wood Thrush Books, and has selected and published the works of several 19th Century writers including *The Laws of Nature: Excerpts from the Writings of Ralph Waldo Emerson*. He lives in Swanton, Vermont with his wife, Judy.

For more information about Walt's books, visit the WTB website: **www.woodthrushbooks.com**

Go to **www.facebook.com\WaltMcLaughlin** to check out his Facebook page, or read his regularly posted blogs at **www.woodswanderer.com**